CONCERT TOUR PRODUCTION MANAGEMENT

How to Take Your Show on the Road

John Vasey

Focal Press

An Imprint of Elsevier

Boston   Oxford   Johannesburg   Melbourne   New Delhi   Singapore

Focal Press is an imprint of Elsevier

Library of Congress Cataloging-in-Publication Data
Vasey, John.
   Concert tour production management / John Vasey.
      p.   cm.
      ISBN-13: 978-0-240-80235-0 ISBN-10: 0-240-80235-7 (alk. paper)
   1. Concert tours—Management—Handbooks, manuals, etc. 2. Popular music—Economic aspects. I. Title.   97-14549
   ML3790.V37   1997   CIP
   780'.78—dc21   MN

ISBN-13: 978-0-240-80235-0
ISBN-10: 0-240-80235-7 (alk. paper)

British Library Cataloguing-in-Publication Data
A catalogue record for this book is available from the British Library.

The publisher offers special discounts on bulk orders of this book. For information, please contact:
Manager of Special Sales
Elsevier
200 Wheeler Road
Burlington, MA 01803
Tel: 781-313-4700
Fax: 781-313-4802

For information on all Focal Press publications available, contact our World Wide Web homepage at http://www.focalpress.com

10 9 8 7
Printed in the United States of America

University Centre Barnsley

CONTENTS

APPENDIX 3

Production Checklists and Forms

APPENDIX 4

Technical Specifications

APPENDIX 5

Vendor Contract

APPENDIX 6

Venue Contract

APPENDIX 7

Translations of Common Terms   153

PREFACE

It is traditional that a book of instruction be filled with rules on how to and how not to, and this book does not follow that tradition. There are no golden rules for the production manager, each production establishes its own set of rules, which continue to evolve for the duration of the tour.

Because every production is original, it has to be treated like a prototype to a certain extent, and the guidelines have to be altered to meet the requirements of each particular production. What works for one tour may not be valid for another, although there may well be several common elements. This book concentrates on the common elements.

This book specifically deals with the business of production and sets out guidelines that have to be followed to get the show on the road. These guidelines have nothing to do with the content of the show, the look, or the sound. They involve the business of making the show happen. The purpose of the book is to provide the basic information to manage the production for a touring concert from start to finish in the most efficient and effective way possible.

Equipment for live concert performances is provided by service companies, commonly known as vendors, that provide sound and lighting equipment or specialize in one or the other. Selection of a particular company depends on location, the performers' artistic requirements, venue size, and most important, the budget. The budget usually sets the limitations for most decisions, so all too often the artistic requirements are trimmed to fit financial necessities. The budget is usually set to fit the popularity of the performers and their ability to draw an audience.

This book begins with an introduction to the touring concert. It explains who's who on the road and where performers' management and agents fit in. Using a production manager's checklists, I take you through a tour with a realistic itinerary that visits different types of venues. I also discuss the role of local promoters' production managers. The larger a crew, the more complex a setup becomes. A small crew can be equally as difficult to coordinate when several tasks are shared among a few persons. It is therefore important that the crew work together as a team. Each person is as important to the success of a show as the next. The technical side of the production is as important as the performance, and it's the production manager who has to coordinate the team and keep their attention on the task at hand in often extremely difficult circumstances. The appendixes provide basic electrical formulas, a performance contract, a technical rider, a production checklist to suit most situations, and several forms that can expedite routine tasks. There is also a glossary of commonly used words.

For those of you who wish to progress to production manager, I hope that this book provides some insight. It does not, however, replace the need for practical experience and taking the bull by the horns.

ACKNOWLEDGMENTS

I would like to thank my wife, Mary, and my daughters, Alice, Lucinda, and Charlotte, for all their support; Sean Hackett for the drawings; Emma Sutherland for research and editing; Sean Moss for the photographs; everyone I have worked with who has helped me accumulate my experience; and everyone who keeps the show on the road.

CHAPTER 1

INTRODUCTION TO THE TOURING CONCERT

REASONS FOR TOURING

A touring concert usually is conducted to perform and promote a recording artist's new material and often coincides with the release of a new compact disc (CD). Some artists like to perform whether or not they have a product to sell; they like the adulation of the audience and the satisfaction of their performance. The areas selected for touring depend on the amount of money offered by the promoters. The amount that a promoter offers depends on the popularity of the artist in the region. This popularity is gauged by the artist's previous accomplishments and current record sales in the region. The agent books the dates with the promoters and often proposes a tour that does not follow any sort of geographic logic. Once a realistic tour is booked and the deals are defined (Figure 1–1), a budget can be set for production. The size and type of venues, the guaranteed fee, and the distance between venues determine the scale of production.

The volume of equipment depends primarily on budget, followed by the artistic requirements of the artist's management, and then of the stars themselves. Unlike theatrical productions in which a producer and a director call the shots, a concert tour is run by the tour manager and the production manager under the direction of the performer's management. Each performer is unique when it comes to touring; they all have their idiosyncrasies.

AUGUST				PAGE
MON	2	DAY OFF/ TRAVEL	ST. PAUL, MN	1
TUE	3	DAY OFF	ST. PAUL, MN	2
WED	4	ROY WILKINS AUDITORIUM	ST. PAUL, MN	3
THU	5	DAY OFF	CHICAGO, IL	4
FRI	6	PINE KNOB MUSIC THEATRE	CLARKSTON, MI	5
SAT	7	WORLD AMPHITHEATER/TINLEY PARK	TINLEY PARK, IL	6
SUN	8	DAY OFF	CHICAGO, IL	7
MON	9	DAY OFF	CHICAGO, IL	8
TUE	10	TRAVEL DAY	CLEVELAND, OH	9
WED	11	NAUTICA STAGE	CLEVELAND, OH	10
THU	12	CELESTE CENTER	COLUMBUS, OH	11
FRI	13	RIVERBEND MUSIC CENTER	CINCINNATI, OH	12
SAT	14	DEER CREEK MUSIC CENTER	NOBLESVILLE, IN	13
SUN	15	TRAVEL DAY	NEW YORK, NY	14
MON	16	DAY OFF	NEW YORK, NY	15
TUE	17	GREAT WOODS AMPHITHEATER	MANSFIELD, MA	16
WED	18	DAY OFF	NEW YORK, NY	17
THU	19	MANN MUSIC CENTER	PHILADELPHIA, PA	18
FRI	20	GARDEN STATE ARTS CENTER	HOLMDEL, NJ	19
SAT	21	JONES BEACH AMPHITHEATER	WANTAUGH, NY	20
SUN	22	DAY OFF	NEW YORK, NY	21
MON	23	MERRIWEATHER POST PAVILION	COLUMBIA, MD	22
TUE	24	STAR LAKE AMPHITHEATER	BURGETTSTOWN, PA	23
WED	25	TRAVEL DAY	CHARLOTTE, NC	24
THU	26	THE PALLADIUM AT CAROWINDS	CHARLOTTE, NC	25
FRI	27	WALNUT CREEK AMPHITHEATER	RALEIGH, NC	26
SAT	28	LAKEWOOD AMPHITHEATER	ATLANTA, GA	27
SUN	29	THE EDGE CONCERT FIELD	ORLANDO, FL	28

Figure 1–1. Schedule from a recent itinerary.

AGENTS, ARTISTS, AND MANAGERS

A band has a manager or manages itself. The manager makes the business decisions regarding record deals, performance fees, media exposure, and legal matters. The manager employs an agent to book shows. The agent works for a commission and usually strives to book to the highest-bidding promoter. The manager has to make sure that the costs of traveling to the shows and providing production do not swallow up the fee, but often this is the case. The manager works with the production manager to schedule shows and to contain production costs in line with fee revenue.

PROMOTERS

The promoter is the entrepreneur who has a feel for the music business and can see an opportunity to make money selling tickets. The promoter makes an offer to the agent for an artist, and often the agent takes bids from several promoters. Competition among promoters goes a lot farther than the amount of money offered. It comes down to experience, history with the artist, and capability to promote through local radio, television, print media, and street posters. Promoters are selling a moment of time. They have the capability to persuade the ticket-buying public that this is the show it has to see.

TOURING ENTOURAGE

PERFORMERS

The performers are the stars of the show. The performers may include a "star," the band, the dancers, and a support act. The performers perform the show, talk to the media, and encourage people to buy their CDs, concert tickets, and merchandising items.

TOUR MANAGER

The tour manager oversees travel arrangements, collects money, pays the bills, and deals with problems as they arise.

PRODUCTION MANAGER

The production manager administers and arranges the technical requirements and staff for the show. These requirements are documented in a contract rider, which is part of the performance contract. The production manager has to have an overview of the entire production to coordinate the touring and local production staff. The very nature of this position requires someone who is unruffled by whatever unexpected situation may arise. A logical mind that can prioritize problems is essential to maintain calm and effective management. The production manager has to be cautious not to exercise too much control and remove the initiative of the production team. The production manager encourages the members of the team to contribute ideas to solve problems and makes it clear that he or she is not there to think for the team. The production manager is the head of all production departments and provides financial and strategic guidance to those departments.

Stage Manager

The stage manager is responsible for allocating the stagehands to the production crew for setup and load out. The stage manager also controls the movement of people and equipment on the stage, which includes cuing venue staff for houselights.

Sound Engineer

The sound engineer operates the front of house (FOH) console, which controls the sound that the audience hears. The sound engineer places the console in an optimum position for the control of the sound system. Often a specific location is reserved for the mixing consoles. This position varies with most venues, but a general position is 90 to 110 feet from the front of the stage.

Monitor Engineer

The monitor engineer operates the monitor console, which controls the sound that the performers hear onstage. The monitor console is positioned at the side of the stage such that gives the engineer a clear line of sight to each performer. The performers rely on the monitor engineer to give each performer the information he or she needs to stay in time and in tune.

Sound Crew

The sound crew works with the sound engineer and monitor engineer to set up and maintain the sound system under the direction of the sound engineer and monitor engineer.

Lighting Operator

The lighting operator operates the control console for the lighting system. The lighting operator may also be the lighting designer, who formulates the overall look of the show and selects type, position, and color of the lighting instruments.

Lighting Crew

The lighting crew sets up, focuses, and maintains the lighting system. When moving lights are used, it is common for specific technicians to handle these instruments. The lighting crew may also be called on to operate curtains, follow spots, smoke machines, or chain hoists during the performance.

Backline Crew

The backline crew is responsible for performers' instruments and equipment, such as guitars, drums, keyboards, and other instruments. The backline crew has the closest relationship with the performers because they maintain their instruments and make the necessary changes during a show.

Set Carpenters

The size of the production may call for set carpenters, who are responsible for risers, flooring, set pieces, curtains, scrims, and props. The set carpenters are the jacks of all trades who build the foundation of the performance space.

Drivers

Truck drivers start work when the show is loaded and finish when they reach the next venue and unload. The crew bus drivers deliver the crew, while they sleep, safely to the next venue.

Other Staff

Some productions may include wardrobe staff, hairdressers, pyrotechnicians, riggers, security personnel, caterers, laser technicians, video crews, and production assistants. A touring entourage can be as small as performers with one crew or expand to include a tour accountant, spouses, children, nannies, massage therapists, personal trainers, publicists, photographers, and other ancillary personnel.

LOCAL PERSONNEL

In addition to the touring party, a large local staff is required for a show.

Promoter

The promoter buys the show from the booking agent and sells the tickets for the show. The promoter also ensures that the requirements set out in the contract rider are met. Sometimes when a promoter plans several shows in different cities, a local representative is employed. The local representative may be sold part or all of the show and take part or all of the risk or profits.

Promoter's Production Manager

The promoter's production manager arranges equipment and staff as required in the contract rider.

Loaders

Loaders unload and reload the trucks (Figure 1–2). They may be union staff with strict breaks and penalty rates if the breaks are not taken within the union guidelines.

Figure 1–2.   Performance area during load in.

Stagehands

The stagehands move equipment into position and assist the touring crew with setup and load out. In some parts of the world, there is no distinction between unloading a truck and loading its contents onto the stage. Stagehands may be union staff with strict guidelines.

Riggers

Riggers attach the chain motors used to lift speakers and lighting trusses to the beams of the building. Riggers may be divided into climbing riggers and ground riggers. When a venue has no suitable rigging points, a ground support system is used for lighting, and the speaker system is stacked on risers or directly onto the stage.

Electrician

The electrician connects the power cables for the sound and lighting equipment to the electrical supply of the venue. Other services may be required depending on the production.

RUNNERS

Runners work under the direction of the production manager; they provide the link to the outside world. Runners are sent out for whatever is required.

SPOTLIGHT OPERATORS

The spotlight operators are required only at show time to operate follow spots, unless there is a specific reason otherwise.

HOUSE LIGHT OPERATOR

The house light operator controls the venue lighting under the direction of the stage manager.

FORKLIFT DRIVER

When a forklift is required, a licensed driver also is required.

CATERERS

The backstage caterers meet the requirements of the contract rider and make sure that the performers and crew are well fed.

VENUE STAFF

The venue staff depends on the size of the audience. The venue staff consists of ticket collectors, ushers, parking attendants, merchandising vendors, and security staff.

DESIGNERS AND OPERATORS

Established performers have a production team that has evolved with them through their careers. The lighting designer and sound engineer are carefully selected by an artist because they are the ones who control the look and sound of the show. In larger productions there may be a set designer, a lighting designer, lighting console operator, and moving light operator. This team works together for the overall look of the performance. The designers get their ideas on paper and made real by the production companies. Once a show is programmed and ready for the road, the designers leave the daily running of the show to the console operators.

CHAPTER 2

THE TOURING
PRODUCTION MANAGER

FROM IDEAS TO REALITY

The beginning of any production is the idea, and there are always several ideas and several opinions. Ideas come from the artists, who explain how they envisage their performance to look and sound. They also come from managers, and they may come from designers appointed by the artist or the artist's manager. Wherever the look comes from, it usually has to go through several stages of approval before the final go ahead is given.

An idea can start as a sketch on a napkin and develop to full blueprints and a scale model (Figure 2–1). Once the creative team agrees on a design, the production manager has the task of working out the costs of building and hiring the elements of the design. The schedule determines the amount of time available to set up for each venue, so the design has to allow setup within those time limitations. The time limitations establish how many crew members are needed and how practical it is to set up and tear down the components of the design. Packaging becomes extremely important to calculate the amount of truck space required. The size and weight of the pieces have to be considered when there are airfreight movements in the schedule.

When the costs are established for building and hiring, the length of the tour and the territories it covers determine whether it is less expensive to rent some parts in each territory or to airfreight the whole lot. These figures also are used to confirm how many crew members are needed to travel everywhere and how many are to be supplied by local vendors.

9

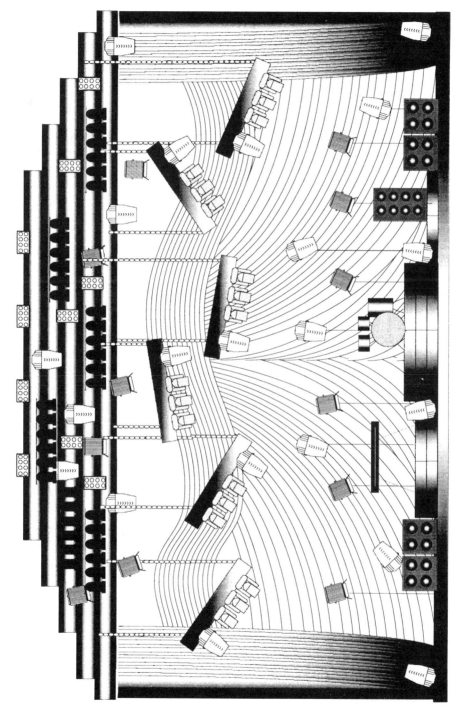

Figure 2–1. An idea at the plan phase. Drawn and designed by Sean "Motley" Hackett.

PREPARING BUDGETS

Preparation of the budget should start with a list of all the materials and staff required. Detailed lists of each component of the sound and lighting equipment have to be sent to vendors for prices. I recommend that these specifications be sent to several vendors to establish a market value for the requirements. Each vendor should be sent the exact same specifications and asked to bid on the same basis, that is, a weekly price or a price for an entire tour.

When at least three separate bids have been obtained from vendors, negotiation begins with the favored vendor. The lowest price is not necessarily the best option. The age and condition of the equipment have to be considered along with the experience of the vendor's staff. The lowest price may come with additional costs in the form of labor-intensive packaging. Inexperienced crews cost time and money with inefficient use of stagehands and loaders at every venue. The condition of the equipment also can cost time during setup when breakdowns occur because of inadequate maintenance. The ability of the vendor to grow with the artist and develop a long-term relationship has to be studied, as do the territories that each vendor can service locally. The efficiency of having consistent production throughout the world has to be weighed against starting from scratch in each new territory with new vendors.

Transportation costs have to be established once the volume of equipment is finalized and the vendors selected. The size and number of trucks can be calculated, then a weekly cost for the driver and truck, then an estimate for fuel and tolls on the basis of the schedule. If there are airfreight moves, the weight and volume of each piece have to be calculated. Airfreight charges are based on a volume-against-weight ratio, this means that although an item may weigh 100 pounds, the size of the item may be such that the volume cost is greater. This ratio is calculated differently by each airline. For international touring a freight agent should be engaged to handle the customs documentation. The document used is called a *carnet* (a document issued by the Chamber of Commerce and Industry, which allows the import and re-export of equipment without paying duties). This document allows the temporary import and export of goods into countries without payment of local taxes and duties. The carnet has to list all the equipment with its value and country of origin. A bond has to be lodged with the issuing office of the carnet. These details are usually handled by the freight agent, so it is important to have a freight agent who is accustomed to dealing with carnet goods.

Crew transportation costs can be planned when the number of crew members is determined. This allows one to decide how many bunks are required in the buses and how many and what size buses are needed. The size and number of buses can be calculated, then a weekly cost for each driver and

Figure 2–2.   Unloading a truck.

bus, then an estimate for fuel and tolls on the basis of the schedule. It is recommended that one obtain at least three quotes for trucks and buses.

Salaries for crew hired directly, such as the stage manager, sound and lighting operators, backline crew, and any other crew not supplied by the vendors have to be negotiated. Per diem expenses also have to be calculated according to the schedule. *Per diem* is the term used for a daily allowance for living away from home, and the expenses are paid in cash each week. The per diem rate may vary with different territories.

Other costs that contribute to the overall production budget are per show expenses. These include consumables (e.g., tape, drum skins, guitar strings), laundry, stagehands, riggers, loaders, follow spot operators, security, catering, and phone and fax costs. These expenses have to be estimated, along with any other locally supplied items or staff that are not part of the promoter's costs.

When all figures are obtained, it is time to meet with the artist's management to approve the budget. This is usually an extremely painful process when management and artist have to confront the reality of the costs. It is then that decisions on what is and is not necessary have to be made and the production scaled to suit the revenue from the performances without putting the artist out of business.

When a tour is doing extremely good business and the logistics of moving the show prevent the show from changing cities overnight, a duplicate of the sound and lighting systems may be required, as may duplicate crews. In this situation a certain number of crew members work every show whereas others work every second show.

BOOKING TOURING STAFF AND EQUIPMENT

It is important to assemble a good team—a crew who can work together and live together on the bus. The sound engineer, monitor engineer, lighting operator, and backline crew need to have the confidence of the artist, because they are the ones directly responsible for the look and sound of the performance.

An experienced crew knows exactly what equipment it wants and what vendors it wants to use. It is up to the production manager to contain the wish list to some form of reality. The crew always wants more than it needs, just in case, but it has to show why it needs a particular item rather than have it rejected because of the budget. A crew does not work well with equipment it regards as inferior or incomplete. Each vendor supplies the crew with equipment. Good production companies can give a tour a great deal of support with good preparation of the equipment and good service on the road. A low hire rate may end up costing more in the long run through equipment failure and poor service on the road.

Although at first sight it appears that the crew is very casual, there is a well-defined hierarchy. The heads of individual departments can instruct their crews to do whatever is needed, but if they require that something be done by another department, they need to approach the head of that department. It is a myth that time is saved when you do something yourself. A piece of equipment moved without the knowledge of the crew responsible may waste more time in an unnecessary search. As in most industries the chain of command has developed over the years. This chain of command has evolved so that those who need to know what is happening do know and can instruct their crew effectively. The worst thing any crew member can do is to involve him- or herself in an area that is not his or her responsibility. This is a total waste of time and is extremely annoying and unprofessional conduct. The production manager may help when asked but must be cautious about offering opinions or advice.

Booking of vendors requires negotiation to confirm exact times for collection of the equipment and crew travel arrangements. Each vendor contract must be carefully examined to make sure all insurance requirements are met for both crew and equipment.

CHAPTER 3

THE PROMOTER'S PRODUCTION MANAGER

The promoter's production manager generally works within one city and handles all the local production requirements for the promoter.

BOOKING STAFF AND EQUIPMENT

The contract rider contains all details that pertain to the show. It details number of crew members required and when they are needed, stage size, rigging points, catering, and other specific requirements. Figure 3–1 shows a production checklist that covers most common requirements. I have used this list in various formats for a number of years to keep track of what and whom I have booked.

Top of Form

VENUE
The name, address, and phone and fax numbers of the venue are entered in this space.

SHOW DATES
The date or dates of the shows are entered.

CAPACITY
The number of seats available for sale is entered. The capacity of a venue depends on the positioning of the stage; sightline restrictions that limit the

iew of the stage caused by speakers, staging, or props; and seats held for mixing and spotlight positions.

CONTACT
The name of the venue technical manager who deals with the venue production staff and other requirements is entered in this space.

DOORS
The door opening time for the audience is specified. Sometimes an audience wants to enter a facility before the door opening time. It is important to have security outside the venue to prevent any pressure on the outside doors. The audience has to be organized into lines so the ticket takers can collect tickets.

SUPPORT
The name of the support act, the name and telephone number of its representative, and the time of its performance are entered.

MAIN
The name, contact, and time of performance for the headline artist are specified.

RIGGING
The time of the rigging call, when the rigging equipment is unloaded and the riggers start work in the roof, is entered. Details of the rigging points are shown on a rigging plot. The plot shows the position of each rigging point in relation to the stage and the weight of the load suspended from the point. The rigging plot also shows the size and type of hoist, such as one-ton motor, two-ton block, rope.

LIGHTS
The time of the lighting load in is specified. This may be the same time as the rigging call, depending on the extent of the setup.

SOUND
The time for the sound load in is specified. The number of cabinets and points is noted.

SET
This is the time the stage set, if there is any, is to be loaded in.

BACKLINE
The backline is equipment such as drums, amplifiers, and keyboards. The time for the backline to be set up is recorded in this space.

VENUE	SHOW DATES		
CAPACITY		DOORS	
CONTACT		SUPPORT	
RIGGING		MAIN	
LIGHTS			
SOUND			
SET			
BACKLINE			
ITEMS	BOOKED	CONFIRMED	COST
STAGE			
STAIRS			
CLEARANCE			
SOUND WINGS			
MIXING POSITION			
CRASH BARRIER			
LOADING ACCESS			
MASKING			
CARPET / MARLEY			
RISERS			
FOLLOW SPOTS			
FORKLIFTS			
CHERRY PICKER			
DRESSING ROOMS			
SIGNAGE			
PYRO /PERMITS			
PHONES			
TOILETS			
OFFICES			
GENERATORS			
WORKLIGHTS			
SOUND POWER			
LIGHTING POWER			
ADDITIONAL POWER			
UTILITY POWER			
CATERING			
VIDEO			
HOUSELIGHTS			
PARKING			
LAUNDRY			
DRY CLEANING			
STAFF			
FOLLOW SPOT OPS			
LOADERS			
PNO TUNA			
SECURITY			
OVERNIGHT SECURITY			
ELECTRICIAN			
RIGGERS			
FORK DRIVERS			
RUNNERS			
WARDROBE			
CARPENTERS			
FIRST AID			

Figure 3–1.   Production checklist.

Items

STAGE

The size and height of the stage are specified in the contract rider. It is important to position the stage on the center line and appropriately for rigging positions. The seating plan determines the limitations of the stage position. The stage must be level, sturdy, and clean. Handrails have to be installed where specified.

STAIRS

The position of stairs is shown on the stage plan supplied with the contract rider. The stairs must have handrails and low-level lights. Each step must have white tape at the edge. When artists leave the stage after performing, they cannot see because of the contrast between the intensity of the lights onstage and the darkness backstage, so the stairs have to be easily identified. Walkways marked with white tape should lead to the stairs.

CLEARANCE

Clearance is the distance between the stage and the rigging points. This dimension identifies any height restrictions with lighting grids or speaker clusters.

SOUND WINGS

Sound wings are required for stacking speakers at the side of the stage when they cannot be flown or it is not necessary for them to be flown. The sound-wing dimensions also accommodate the monitor engineer and control equipment. The sound wing also may be the position for guitar technicians and other backline crew. Even when the main speaker clusters are flown, there is still a requirement for ground-stacked speakers. These may be stacked directly on the floor or may require a platform.

MIXING POSITION

The site of the mixing consoles must be determined. The size and height of the risers required for the mixers are specified in the rider—generally a central position about 90 to 110 feet from the front of the stage. The seats behind the mixing position have to be held out because of the obstruction caused by the consoles and the operators.

CRASH BARRIER

A crash barrier is required for acts that generate a great deal of excitement among young fans. The barrier has to be guarded by trained security staff who know how to handle overexcited teenagers without violence. A mosh pit also may be required. This is a fenced area in front of the stage used to separate large audiences. The barrier line of the mosh pit also must be competently guarded.

LOADING ACCESS

How the equipment enters the building and gets to the stage must be defined. Access may be as simple as a loading dock at stage level or as complicated as unloading a truck in the street and moving equipment through an exit door, along a passageway, up two floors in an elevator, along another passageway, and taking a fork onto the stage. Sometimes access can be even worse, involving cross-loading equipment onto smaller trucks and moving it up or down stairs and through mud, snow, and ice.

MASKING

Drapes may be required to mask unused parts of an arena, such as scoreboards, seats, conflicting signage, or unsightly walls.

CARPET/MARLEY

The covering for the stage floor must be specified. Most tours carry the preferred stage flooring. The most common floors are Marley or Harlequin flooring, which is like linoleum that comes in six-foot-wide rolls. The floor covering rolls out flat and is kept in place with tape. Carpet is also commonly used for its acoustic benefits.

RISERS

The need for platforms on which to set drums and keyboards must be determined. Most bands tour with their own risers. Risers usually are needed for festival-type events in which the risers have to be on wheels to accelerate set changes. Risers may be required for wheelchair seating when no such facilities are provided at a venue.

FOLLOW SPOTS

The number and type of follow spotlights required is specified in the rider. If the venue does not have them, suitable spotlights have to be supplied by a local vendor. The production manager has to know the position of the spotlights and the access to this position before booking the spotlights.

FORKLIFTS

The number and type of forklifts is specified in the rider. The forklifts should be in good working order with spare fuel readily available. A forklift with a punctured tire or no fuel is an extremely frustrating sight.

CHERRY PICKER

Some venues have no access to the rigging points other than from below. This is when a cherry picker is needed. Cherry pickers also are called boom arm lifts.

DRESSING ROOMS

The number of dressing rooms required depends on the number of acts in the show. Dressing room allocation has a pecking order; main act takes first pick then the support acts choose.

SIGNAGE

The show may be sponsored, and signage may be necessary. The placement of signs may be restricted to outside the auditorium in the foyers and entrances. Signs in the auditorium may have to be covered or removed to comply with artists' sponsorship commitments.

PYROTECHNICS/PERMITS

Permits are required for any pyrotechnics in most cities. The fire marshal has to be notified, and a list of effects being used has to be submitted. Sometimes the fire marshals may ask to see the effects before giving approval. Other permits required depend on city regulations. Fire-proofing certificates may be required for any drapes. Other permits include barricade permits, rigging permits, temporary electrical installation permits, and parking permits.

TELEPHONES

Production office phone and fax numbers to be used for the event have to be booked with the local telephone company if the venue cannot supply the requirements.

TOILETS

There must be enough toilet facilities for the production staff.

OFFICES

The production office is the hub of any production. It is where orders originate and decisions are made. An office convenient to the stage and catering is standard. Other offices are required for tour managers, tour accountants, and personal assistants.

GENERATORS

Generators are required when the venue does not have sufficient electrical supply for the production. It is important to monitor fuel use and have someone specifically responsible for the generators. Like any diesel motor, generators can stop if they are not properly maintained.

WORKLIGHTS

It is important to check the position and working order of the worklights before nightfall. Loading docks have to be well lit for the load out.

SOUND POWER

Three-phase electrical service is dedicated to the sound system. The capacity of this service is documented in the rider.

LIGHTING POWER

Three-phase electrical service is dedicated to the lighting system. The capacity of this service is documented in the rider.

ADDITIONAL POWER

Electrical power is needed for other services, such as video, lasers, and hydraulics.

UTILITY POWER

Power is required for services such as catering and wardrobe.

CATERING

The catering requirements are specified in the rider. These requirements cover crew meals, band dressing rooms, after-show food and drinks, and bus food and drinks. The time and number of meals ordered should be recorded here.

VIDEO

Some venues supply in-house video reinforcement, and some artists tour with video. This section of the form is for video requirements such as camera positions, screen positions, and projector positions.

HOUSELIGHTS

Houselights are the venue lighting when the audience has arrived. The control of houselights is important to the mood of a concert. A concert auditorium does not have to be lit like a sports arena. I usually set the houselights to bright when the doors open, not so bright at intermission, and bright at the end. The position of the houselight control and the communication to the houselight operator must be defined.

PARKING

Permits may be required to unload trucks at some venues let alone park them. The parking of tour vehicles can be difficult at inner-city venues. After trucks and buses are unloaded, they may have to go to a parking lot and return at the end of the show. It is far more convenient when there is space to park the tour trucks and buses backstage. When there is space at the venue, power is required for the buses.

LAUNDRY

There is always laundry with any tour. It may be limited to a handful of stage clothes or extend to large numbers of costumes. The number of machines, whether they require coins, and their location should be determined.

DRY CLEANING

When there is a requirement for dry cleaning, the location of a suitable dry cleaner has to be determined. The dry cleaner must be advised of the rush job needed on show day. The need for towels is always included on a rider. Towels are needed for crew showers, for the stage, for the dressing rooms, and for the support acts. Towels can be supplied by hotels when a reasonable number is required. A linen service can be used when a large number is necessary.

Staff

FOLLOW SPOT OPERATORS

Follow spot operators control both front of house (FOH) follow spots and truss follow spots. The truss follow spots are on the lighting trusses above the stage. Follow spot operators have to be trained to use the light and to follow cues. The truss operators need to be able to climb rope ladders to the truss and climb along the truss to the spot chair. Truss spot operators are required to wear black clothes and shoes.

LOADERS

Loaders unload equipment from the trucks. The loaders may also work as stagehands. The number of loaders to be booked is specified in the rider. Some unions may specify the number of loaders based on the number of trucks.

PIANO TUNER

When an acoustic piano is used in a performance, a piano tuner is needed. The piano tuner requires the minimum of background noise. I generally try to book the piano tuner at the same time as the lighting focus when the sound crew has gone to lunch. The piano may have to be retuned each day because of temperature fluctuations during a show.

SECURITY

The number of security personnel required depends on the type of audience an act attracts. Security staff should be booked for a briefing by the touring production manager before they go to their positions. Every act has its own way of dealing with overly enthusiastic fans.

OVERNIGHT SECURITY

Overnight security is required for consecutive shows in the same venue. Even though there is building security, a dedicated guard or guards should be assigned to watch over the stage and dressing rooms. Overnight security should be maintained until the production crew arrives in the afternoon.

ELECTRICIAN

The electrician is required to connect the sound and lighting systems to the venue power service. This connection is usually made with a set of three-phase tails. The tails are connected to the venue distribution board and then to the sound and lighting distribution systems. A licensed electrician is required to make three-phase connections.

RIGGERS

The riggers attach chain motors to the beams in the roof of the venue. The number of riggers required depends on the number of points, the position of the points in relation to the roof beams, and the time available to complete the rigging. Each venue has to be staffed accordingly. The rigging crew includes climbing riggers and ground riggers. The climbing riggers work in the roof, and the ground riggers prepare and attach the slings to the chain motors (Figure 3–2).

FORKLIFT OPERATORS

Forklift operators have to be licensed operators. The forklifts have to work among a large number of people, and there is no place for antics. Forklifts can be extremely dangerous, and extreme caution is necessary.

RUNNERS

Runners need to have good knowledge of local music shops, laundries, restaurants, and so on, and they must have a mobile phone. Runners are the link to the outside world for the production crew. The runners have to have the initiative to cover the loose ends that develop as part of staging a concert.

WARDROBE

Wardrobe staff are required for washing, ironing, and dressing for some productions.

CARPENTERS

A separate crew of carpenters may be required for the stage set. Carpenters work at different pay scales from stagehands and loaders.

Figure 3–2.   Bolting the trussing together.

STAGEHANDS

Stagehands take equipment from truck to stage and assist the touring crew in setup. Stagehands also may unload the trucks in places where no distinction is made between loaders and stagehands. The number of stagehands required is specified in the rider. The number of stagehands may have to be increased from rider specifications at venues with difficult access.

FIRST AID

A first aid team is needed for most concerts. The first aid station has to be easily accessible from the crash barrier. The first aid team has to be in place before the doors open.

PREPARING A VENUE

Before the touring production team arrives, the venue must be ready. This means that at least half an hour before the scheduled start time the lights are on, catering is set up and ready to go, the production office has telephones, keys for dressing rooms and offices are in hand, loading docks are open, and the stage is ready. The rows of seats directly in front of the stage have to be stacked out of the way of any rigging points, and the mixing risers have to be set in position. All local staff should sign in and be ready to start at the scheduled time; they must not arrive at or after the scheduled start time.

PUBLIC SAFETY

The safety of the public should be of concern to the production manager. Barricades in front of the stage and around the mixing consoles to protect the audience from the equipment and the stars from the audience must be structurally sound and set appropriately for the type of act performing.

Working in the live music industry exposes one to hazards and risks. To ensure safety and reduce risk to the vanishing point, a safety assessment has to be done as a matter of routine before any task is begun. Most safety regulations cite reasonable and practical precautions. The safety of staff, artists, and the paying public has to be considered at all times. Safety ultimately is a matter of caution mixed with common sense. Learn first aid!

Electrical Safety

Always meter supply before connection.

Always isolate the supply before connection.

Never replace a fuse with one of greater value.

Never disconnect grounds.

Always lay excess cable in a figure eight, never coiled in a circle.

Rigging Safety

Never stand under a moving load.

Always wear a harness when working at heights.

Learn how to tie knots efficiently.

Never stand directly under riggers working overhead.

Never use frayed or damaged slings.

Always double-check all rigging procedures.

Always secure tools to your harness when working at heights.

Fire Safety

Never block fire exits or fire equipment.

Always check smoke detectors before using smoke machines.

Know the position of the nearest extinguishers.

Sound-Level Safety

Prolonged exposure to high sound levels can cause hearing loss. The recommended maximum audience exposure in the United Kingdom is 104 adjusted decibels over the duration of the event. Hearing protection should be worn by persons exposed to high sound levels for long periods.

Public Safety

Never leave electrical connections in public areas unsupervised.

Never expose an audience to any danger.

Always make sure that equipment is kept secure from the public.

CHAPTER 4

GETTING THE SHOW ON THE ROAD

PRODUCTION REHEARSALS

The plans have been discussed for weeks, maybe months, and changed several times as part of the development to the rehearsal stage. Everything should work according to plan. This does happen, but all too often there are hiccups that do not appear on the plans. The whole setup is like one huge jigsaw puzzle, and when any one thing changes it can affect several other things. The true test is to set everything as per the plans to program lighting and rehearse a show.

The musicians should have rehearsed the music in a small rehearsal room before production rehearsals so that the time for production rehearsals can be used to integrate the musicians to the technical side of the show to produce stunning entertainment. The production rehearsal period should be used to mark clearly as many elements of the equipment as possible. This reduces setup time dramatically. All equipment cases should be color coded according to destination at the venue, that is, onstage, stage left, stage right, front of house (FOH). All cases also should be marked with their contents and weight. Truck loading can be simplified by means of color coding for each truck. The order of packing can be identified with numbering of each case.

The sound, lighting, and backline crews should have as many cables as possible loomed together and labeled clearly. This reduces patching time, because patching often has to be done with limited lighting and space in dark corners on and under the stage. All cable labeling should have a logical sequence that can be easily followed.

Rehearsal time also should be used to get the crew working together as a team. The setup schedule should be discussed with the crew chiefs from each department so that everyone knows when there is going to be noise and when there will be darkness. The sequence of the setup should be worked out so that there is no double handling of equipment, which is both boring and time consuming. Time taken for a brief meeting with all the crew chiefs saves arguments or discussions during setup.

TRAVEL AND ACCOMMODATION

Travel and accommodation are booked by the tour manager. It is in the interest of the production manager to go through the hotel and travel arrangements with the tour manager to make sure the tour manager understands the production schedule. The hotels should be sent a list of instructions to facilitate check in. The following are sample instructions to be sent to a hotel.

Security Measures

Under no circumstance should hotel staff give out any information regarding this group, using real or assumed names.

Preregistration

Please preregister the entire group and have room keys and a copy of the rooming list in a sealed envelope for each group member on arrival. Please include a hotel information sheet with a full list of features and facilities.

Rooming Lists

Please use only the supplied rooming list. Under no circumstances should any other information be supplied on the list.

Arrival and Departure

Please provide at least two porters on arrival with at least two luggage carts to assist with baggage. The group will assign someone to assist with the distribution of luggage. Please make sure that the porters have an accurate copy of the rooming list for the whole party with baggage tag numbers clearly marked on it.

Housekeeping

Housekeeping must honor the "*Do Not Disturb*" signs unquestioningly. They must not try to verify occupancy or check minibars by knocking, phoning, entering, or trying to enter the group rooms.

THE FINE PRINT

HERE WE GO AGAIN, BUT BEFORE WE DO, HERE ARE A FEW THINGS THAT WILL BE COVERED AT THE END OF THE TOUR QUIZ (WORTH 60% OF YOUR FINAL GRADE). REMEMBER, SPELLING COUNTS.

1. ALL THE INFORMATION CONTAINED IN THESE PAGES SEEMED PRETTY ACCURATE WHEN WE WERE ASSEMBLING IT, BUT WE'VE ALWAYS BEEN TOO TRUSTING AND IT IS ENTIRELY POSSIBLE THAT SOME OF THE TELEPHONE NUMBERS OR HOURS OF ROOM SERVICE BEAR VERY LITTLE RESEMBLANCE TO REALITY. FOR THAT WE SAY, "WE'RE SORRY", FOR THAT WE SAY, "PLEASE FORGIVE US", FOR THAT WE SAY, "GET OVER IT AND GET ON THE BUS". WE'LL GET YOU ANY NEW INFORMATION AS SOON AS WE GET IT. WE'RE LIKE THAT.

2. LAMINATED PASSES ARE FOR TOURING STAFF ONLY. TO HELP THWART INFILTRATION FROM UNAUTHORIZED PERSONNEL, ASTRAL PROJECTORS, OR OUT OF WORK SOVIET SCIENTISTS. ALL GUESTS WILL BE ISSUED DAY OF SHOW PASSES. PLEASE ADVISE YOUR GUESTS THAT A GUEST PASS DOES NOT ALLOW THEM TO PHOTOGRAPH THE SHOW.

3. ALL GUEST LISTS WILL BE CLOSED AT 6:00 PM ON SHOW DAYS OR WHEN THE ALLOTMENT IS USED UP. WE HAVE A LIMITED NUMBER OF TICKETS IN EACH VENUE AND THEY DO COST US MONEY SO DON'T FEEL OBLIGATED TO INVITE EVERYONE YOU PASSED IN THE HOTEL LOBBY ON YOUR WAY TO THE GIG. A GUEST PASS ALONE WILL NOT ALLOW THAT PERSON INTO THE VENUE. THEY MUST HAVE A TICKET AS WELL. ANY PRE-SHOW GUESTS WILL BE ASKED TO RETURN TO THEIR SEATS 20 MINUTES BEFORE THE START OF THE PERFORMANCE. AFTER SHOW GUESTS WILL NOT BE ALLOWED BACKSTAGE UNTIL 15 MINUTES AFTER THE END OF THE SHOW, AND OF COURSE NO GUESTS ARE PERMITTED ON STAGE, BUT YOU KNEW THAT.

5. YOU AND YOU ALONE ARE RESPONSIBLE FOR TAKING CARE OF ANY HOTEL INCIDENTAL CHARGES. EVEN IF YOU THINK YOU DON'T HAVE ANY, PLEASE MAKE SURE YOU CHECK OUT AT THE FRONT DESK. ANY INCIDENTAL CHARGES NOT PAID WILL COME BACK TO HAUNT YOU AND YOU WILL BE SHUNNED BY YOUR FRIENDS AND FAMILY.

WE REALIZE THAT YOU KNEW ALL THIS ALREADY, BUT WE'RE GLAD WE HAD THIS LITTLE CHAT.

THANKS TOO MUCH,
MR. LOAD IN

Figure 4–1.   Introduction to a recent itinerary.

Room Allocation

Absolutely no construction work must be conducted in or around the hotel. Please check locally before our arrival to assure that no such work is under way or is scheduled to start before our departure. All rooms should be allocated away from any sources of noise such as elevators, main roads, stairways, ice and vending machines, housekeeping stations, or staff rest areas. All rooms should have king-size beds. Please try to allocate all rooms on the same floor when possible unless otherwise advised.

Accounts

If signatures are required on registration cards, folios, or other documents, the tour manager is authorized to sign on behalf of all group members. Please set up a master folio for all room and tax charges. Please set up a separate folio for each room, listing incidental charges only. These charges are to be paid directly by each guest on departure.

Legibility

Please mark each folio with complete names and room numbers to avoid confusion at check out or with late charges.

Form of Payment

The tour manager will pay all room charges on departure by means of either company check or company credit card. Please make up one master folio for all rooms and have the list ready for the tour manager to check the night before check out. If all instructions for rooming lists, check out, and payment details are followed, it will expedite group movement in your reception area and alleviate problems at check out.

Communications

DAY SHEETS

The tour manager will issue day sheets to all members of the group. These day sheets are to be placed under the door of each room by your porters promptly after the sheet has been given to reception. This will typically be between 11 P.M. and 1 A.M.

TELEPHONE CALLS

Under no circumstances should a call be transferred to any room unless the name used on the rooming list is given.

THURSDAY, AUGUST 12   **COLUMBUS, OH**
CELESTE CENTER   **EASTERN TIME**

TRAVEL

BAND: ⎫ DEPART LOBBY AT 11:30 PM FOR COLUMBUS, OH
              ⎬ 140 MILES - 3 HOURS
CREW: ⎭

HOTEL   **BAND**   **CREW**
             GUEST QUARTERS   NONE
             50 S. FRONT STREET
             COLUMBUS, OH 43215

         ☎ 614/228-4600
    FAX: 614/228-0297
    CTC: JULIA HANSEN
TO VENUE: 25 MINUTES

             DRIVERS
             GUEST QUARTERS
             50 S. FRONT STREET
             COLUMBUS, OH 43215

         ☎ 614/228-4600
    FAX: 614/228-0297
TO VENUE: JULIA HANSEN
TO VENUE: 25 MINUTES

VENUE   CELESTE CENTER
             717 E 17TH AVENUE
             COLUMBUS, OH 43211

    MAIN#: 614/644-4534   **DOORS:**
    FAX #: 614/644-4144   **MIDNIGHT OIL:**
   PROD #: 614/644-4177
    FAX #: 614/644-4685   **CAPACITY:** 10,299

PROMOTER: OHIO EXPOSITION CENTER / PROMO WEST
              130 E CHESTNUT ST.
              COLUMBUS, OH 432311

     TEL #: 614/641-6285
     FAX #: 614/462-6271

AFTER SHOW TRAVEL

         BAND: STAY OVER

       CREW: DEPART FOR CINCINNATI, OH
                                  110 MILES - 3 MILES

NOTES

Figure 4–2.   A day on the road.

CORRESPONDENCE

Should, for any reason, letters, packages, or parcels be delivered to your hotel in advance of our arrival, they must be held in a secure place and handed to the tour manager on arrival. If anything arrives after the group's departure please notify the travel agent immediately for further instructions. *Do not* send any packages back to the sender. Your efforts and attention to the foregoing details are much appreciated.

ADAPTING THE SHOW TO DIFFERENT VENUES

It is inevitable that at some point a show will not fit into the venue. Some adaptations have to be made to make it work because the stage is too narrow, too low, or too short, the clearance is not high enough, or there is a fire curtain right where the lighting grid sits. There may not be enough power, dressing rooms, or space. All these problems and more have to become challenges, because whatever the situation, the production team is expected to deliver a show to an audience that night. To minimize the drama of a difficult setup, notice should be given to all crew that amendments to the standard setup have to be made and what those changes are. This communication reduces conflict in what will be difficult circumstances.

CHAPTER 5

ADVANCING VENUES

PRELIMINARY CONTACT

Before the tickets for a show go on sale, the production manager reviews sightline restrictions, stage size and position, mixing size and position, barricades, and any other production element that affects seating.

DETAILED ADVANCE

The production manager makes detailed advance arrangements with the technical manager of the venue as soon as the details of the show are determined. A checklist is customized to the contract rider to make sure every requirement is covered, because requirements vary from act to act. Once it has been established whether there are any problems setting up a show in a particular venue, the production manager can start to work on amending the setup to the venue.

FINAL CHECK

A final check is done the day before each new setup to make sure the local staff is ready for the show and to deal with any last-minute changes.

Figure 5–1. Loading the truck.

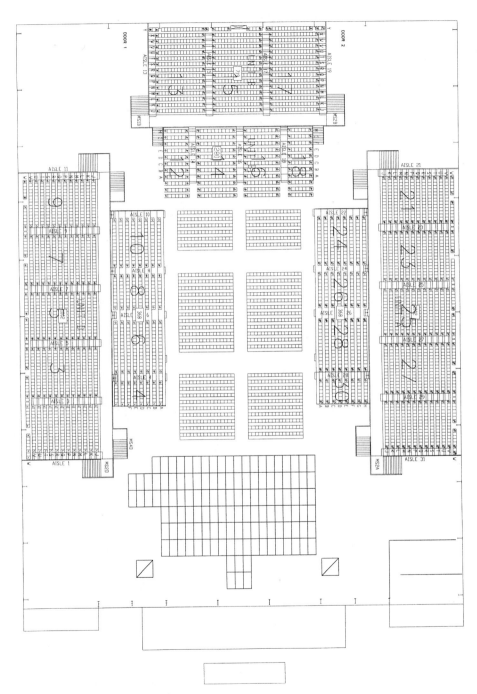

Figure 5–2.   Venue seating plan.

CHAPTER 6

DAILY SCHEDULE

A SHOW DAY

The following is an example of a call sheet for setup and show the same day. This type of schedule is typical of a touring show that sets up in six different cities a week. The number of crew members needed to maintain the schedule varies according to size of production and start time. Setup for smaller productions starts later and may also finish later. Large productions may require earlier rigging calls or extra setup days.

8:00 A.M.	Rigging and lighting crew
10:00 A.M.	Sound and set crew
12:00 NOON	Backline crew
2:00 P.M.	Lighting focus
3:30 P.M.	Sound EQ (equalizer)
4:30–5:30 P.M.	Sound check headline act
6:00 P.M.	Support sound check
7:00 P.M.	Doors open
8:00–8:45 P.M.	Support act
8:45–9:15 P.M.	Changeover
9:15–11:00 P.M.	Headline act
11:00 P.M.	Load out

The schedule for the production manager would be as follows.

7:00 A.M.

Get out of bed, your bunk on the bus, and get showered and ready for another day of excitement.

7:30 A.M.

Make sure the catering is ready, the venue is open, and the lights are on. Wake up the truck drivers and get the trucks into position ready to unload. Meet the promoter's production manager for a tour of the venue entrances, facilities, and dressing rooms. Meet with the local crew chief and allocate crew members to the various departments, such as sound and lighting. Meet with the technical manager for the venue and check that all the phones are connected in the office as per the numbers in the itinerary. Set up the production office. Before the truck is unloaded, the desks and chairs can be arranged for the production office case to come off the truck. The touring riggers mark out the points for the venue riggers.

8:00 A.M.

Stagehands, loaders, and riggers start work, and the equipment begins to roll off the trucks. The climbing riggers go to the roof and the ground riggers start to prepare the slings. The lighting crew begins to get its trusses into place and join the sections together. While the chain motors are being rigged, the lighting crew attaches them to the trusses. When the production office case makes it to the office, the fax machine can be connected, and signs can be hung for the dressing rooms and directions to the stage. During this time the electrician connects the lighting power cables to the venue supply. When all the lighting cases are out of the truck, the stagehands work under the direction of the lighting crew to get the trusses up and out of the way of the stage as quickly as possible. By now the office can be fully functional. I use clipboards for all routine forms, such as runners' lists, time sheets, accounts to be paid. The sound crew should be up and about ready for its call.

10:00 A.M.

The sound crew leaps into action and works with the stagehands to put the speakers into place. The set crew takes its carts off the trucks and prepares to place them on the stage as soon as the lighting trusses are high enough to start assembling the set. The set may be a simple drum riser, but the same principle applies: get the trusses up to head height as soon as possible so that other work can continue on the stage. When the lighting trusses are raised, the cables from the lamps are patched into the dimmers. The production office is quiet at this time, and the production manager can do some advance work.

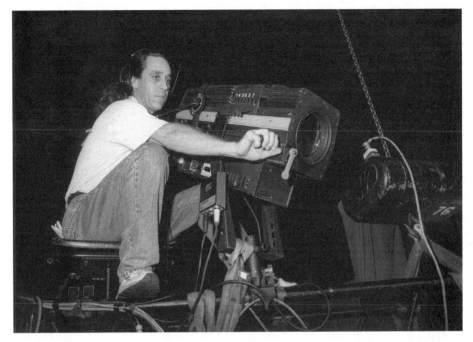

Figure 6–1.   Operating a truss spotlight.

When the advance work is thorough, setup runs without the production manager's continually being asked for assistance. This leaves time to deal with unexpected problems.

NOON

The backline crew begins to set up the instruments. If the stage is not ready, the crew can prepare the guitar tuning stations, arrange the dressing room, and take drums and drum stands out of the cases and ready them to be put on stage. When the trusses are out of the way, the lighting crew takes a lunch break. The sound crew can set up the monitor system and front of house (FOH) consoles and place the microphones on the stands ready to go onto the stage when the backline crew has its equipment ready.

2:00 P.M.

The lighting focus is a good time for the sound, set, and backline crews to have lunch. The focus requires little or no other light than the particular instruments being focused. This makes any other task on stage difficult without a flashlight. The lighting focus can be done quickly if the lighting crew is organized. Communication between the console operator and the crew on the trusses focusing the lamps has to be clear. The lighting crew member who is

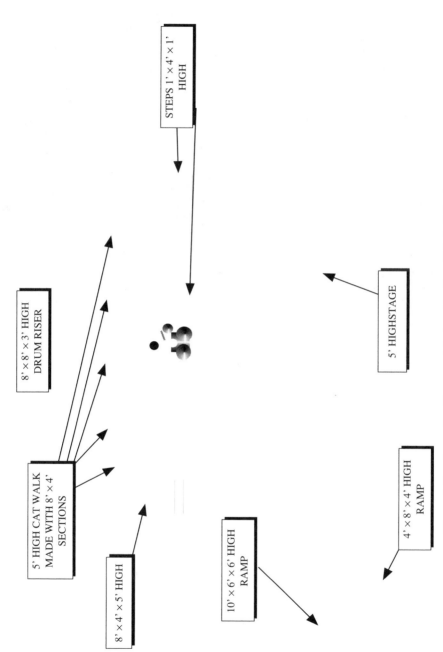

Figure 6–2. Stage plan. Drawn and designed by Sean "Motley" Hackett.

directing the focus has a planned sequence to focus. This planned sequence minimizes the amount of backtracking on the trusses. The production manager issues passes to local crew and venue staff who need backstage access.

3:30 P.M.
This is a good time for everyone to leave the building. The sound equalization process can be extremely annoying to anyone in the vicinity. Pink noise generally is used to analyze the acoustics of a venue. This is followed by several minutes of "one, two" by the sound engineer and music played at show volume. The sound engineer walks the venue to check the coverage of the speaker system with music at show level. The bigger the venue the longer this takes. The dressing rooms are prepared for the arrival of the musicians.

4:00 P.M.
The musicians and tour manager arrive for the sound check. The production manager greets them and shows them to the dressing room. The sound and backline crews conduct a line check. This entails checking each microphone and setting levels and tone in both FOH and monitor systems.

4:30 P.M.
The sound check procedure starts. The general procedure is to check each musician and then the entire group. The drummer generally has the most channels on a console and takes the longest to check. The time this takes can be reduced if the crew can set the level and tone before the musicians arrive; then only slight adjustments need to be made.

5:30 P.M.
When the headline act has finished its sound check the support act conducts a sound check. The backline crew moves as little as possible to allow space for the support act to set up. The support act has its own backline crew and sound and lighting operators. If they do not have their own operators, they usually use vendor crews for a negotiated fee.

6:00 P.M.
When the support act is set up and ready, it goes through the sound check process. This can sometimes be more difficult than a headline act sound check because of inexperienced backline crew and inexperienced musicians. Today's support act may be tomorrow's headline act, so all support acts have to be given a chance. The production manager has to make sure the venue is ready to open and the security staff has been briefed before going to its positions. The houselights should be set at an appropriate level. The guest list is taken to the ticket office.

7:00 P.M.

Doors open and the audience flocks in and takes its seats. Appropriate music is playing to set the mood as the audience enters.

8:00–8:45 P.M.

The support act plays its set.

8:45–9:15 P.M.

Changeover is the term used for removal of the support act's equipment and resetting for the headline act. This involves stagehands, backline crew, and sound crew. The sound crew goes through a line-check procedure whereby each audio line is checked to make sure that nothing has broken down since sound check. Music is played to set the mood for the headline act.

9:15–11:00 P.M.

The headline act performs its set. Before the end of the show, the production manager goes through stagehand allocation with the local crew chief.

11:00 P.M.

Load out begins. The aim is to take the show down and load the equipment in the trucks as quickly and safely as possible. Most crews work a minimum of three hours, so I generally hire enough local crew to take the show down within three hours. To achieve the speed and efficiency of working within time limitations, the crew needs plenty to drink. Water and other nonalcoholic beverages should be readily available so that crew members do not have to leave the work area to get a drink. It is important that the touring crew be organized for the load out. Crew members should know where their empty equipment cases are, how many stagehands they have to assist them, and the jobs that the stagehands are supposed to be doing. When a show has to move extraordinary distances and time is tight, the local crew should be increased to facilitate the load out. When the trucks are loaded, the crew takes showers and returns to the bus.

A TRAVEL DAY

Traveling anywhere can be full of adventure. One never knows what is around the corner. On the bus, the bus driver gets everyone where they are going. Traveling from city to city by plane, one has to deal with the congestion of the cities and endless walks through airline terminals with luggage. I recommend never taking on tour any more than one can carry oneself.

A DAY OFF ──

(This space is left blank for one's imagination.)

PERFORMANCE CONTRACT

[The following is an example of a performance contract used for a concert.]

This rider (hereinafter called "the rider") forms part of and is to be constructed with the Agreement between _____ (the "Company") and _____ (the "Promoter") dated _____ ("the Concert Agreement") for the services of the band _____ ("the band") to perform at _____ ("the hall") on the _____ ("the engagement").

If there is any inconsistency between the provisions of the rider and the provisions of the Agreement, the provisions of the rider shall prevail. The rider and the Concert Agreement as amended by time provisions of the rider shall be hereinafter referred to as "the Agreement."

CANCELLATION

The Company reserves the right to terminate the Agreement in the following events:

1. If the sound engineer, lighting director, tour manager, or any member of the band dies or becomes incapacitated for any reason;

2. If performance of any of the Company's obligations hereunder shall render the band, Company, or Company's employers or agents liable to civil proceedings; or,

3. If in the Company's absolute discretion performance of the Agreement shall expose the band, any employee of the Company, or any third-party

contractor hired by the Company to the possibility or death or injury or if the Company's performance of the Agreement shall become impossible as a result of riot, civil strife, or any other event that renders the engagement unduly difficult to perform.

If the Agreement is terminated by the Company by reason of any of the above terms, then the Company shall refund to the Promoter any amounts paid to the Company pursuant to the Agreement, but the Company shall not be further liable in any event for any other loss or damage suffered by the Promoter as a result of such termination.

ADVERTISING

1. The band shall receive 100 percent sole star billing in all advertising in respect of the engagement. The Promoter's name and the name of the venue in which the engagement shall be performed shall not appear on any ticket, advertising, or publicity larger than 20 percent of the size of print used in the band's name.

2. If the venue has a marquee, then the name of the band must appear on such marquee on the night of each performance.

3. The Promoter will notify all radio stations' traffic and accounting offices that all electronic media buys placed by promoters or advertising agencies for all of the band's tour dates are to be treated as co-op purchase and payments. Piggyback or dual talent spots are unacceptable and will not be allowed for payment. The Company's representative may contact each advertising station in advance of the performance.

4. All invoicing presented at settlement for payment must be original and must contain the following:
    a) Gross, net, and commissionable or discountable amounts
    b) A notarized affidavit of performance (through two days prior to event) stating dates run, times run, and contract rates
    c) Co-presents packages detailed in letter form by a station official and notarized
    d) An invoice number dated with band listed as the client

5. Agency orders will not be approved for payments.

6. Original tear sheets must accompany all invoicing for print advertising.

7. Radio station ticket giveaways or trades can be done only with the Company's written approval. If this approval is granted, the tickets can be given only in exchange for spots on a one-to-one basis, that is, one hundred $10 tickets in exchange for $1000 in radio time invoiced. In this eventuality an original invoice from the participating station must be presented during

settlement, along with the written approval confirmation and the complimentary ticket (comp) sheet from the box office.

8. Poster and/or flyer invoices are governed by above, and delivery invoicing must have location address where dispersed.

9. Approved radio spots are allowed for payment.

PERMITS AND LICENSING

1. All permits, licenses, or authorizations of any kind required by any union, public authority, performing rights society, or any other legitimate third party shall be obtained by the Promoter at his/her sole cost, and the Promoter at the request of the Company shall furnish licenses to the Company. This requirement includes driving permits where necessary for the Company and its transport contractors.

2. It is of the essence of this Agreement that the Promoter shall use his/her best endeavors to ensure that no audio or visual recordings are made of any performances undertaken by the band in accordance with this Agreement. If any representative of the Company becomes aware of professional audio or visual recording equipment being taken into the venue or used during the performance then he/she shall bring it to the attention of the Promoter, who shall immediately confiscate the equipment and eject the persons responsible from the venue. Failure by the Promoter to do this immediately upon request by the Company's representative shall entitle the Company to terminate the performance immediately, and the Company shall be entitled to the full fee for the performance.

THE PERFORMANCE

1. The band will perform one performance per day, and such performance shall be played without an interval.

2. The performance will last between 80 and 150 minutes, but it is acknowledged by all parties that the playing time is uncertain and will at all times be under the control of the Company. However, the Promoter will use his/her best endeavors to ensure that everything under his/her control is correctly arranged so that the performance can start on time.

3. All matters of performance production shall be controlled by the tour manager or his/her representative on behalf of the Company, and the tour manager shall decide the decibel level; however, the Promoter must inform the production manager of any local laws relating to permitted decibel levels or curfew times.

4.   The band's performance does not require a master of ceremonies or an announcer, and no such person shall be employed without the prior written consent of the Company.

5.   All negotiations with union representatives, fire chief, police chief, hall manager, and any other authorities in respect to overtime or any additional payments must be completed by the Promoter at least one hour before the performance and the result of such negotiation conveyed to the Company's representative.

6.   The Promoter shall ensure that it is safe for the band to perform on stage. If any missiles that may endanger the safety of the band or stage crew are thrown onto the stage during a performance, then the band in its absolute discretion shall be entitled to terminate the show, in which case the Promoter shall still be liable for the full fee due under the Agreement.

SUPPORT ACT

1.   No other act ("Support Act") may appear on the same program without the prior written consent of the Company.

2.   If a support act is used then the band shall have the first right to set up all instruments and equipment used in the performance, and such instruments and equipment shall not be moved or used by anyone other than the tour manager or production manager or anyone at their direction.

3.   The support act shall not appear on any advertising without the prior written consent of the Company.

4.   The band shall be entitled to a sound check for at least two hours before the official time of the opening of the venue doors to the public.

PAYMENT

Payment of the guaranteed fee and percentages as set out in the Concert Agreement shall be made as follows:

1.   Fifty percent (50%) of the said guaranteed fee shall be deposited with the Company's agent as follows: ten percent (10%) upon signing the Agreement and the balance of forty percent (40%) fifteen (15) days before the performance.

2.   The balance of the said fee and percentages must be paid by check upon settlement of the receipts and expenses (as set out below) on the day of the performance. If the tour manager so requests, part of or all of the balance shall be paid in cash.

With respect to performances for which the Company is being paid on the basis of a percentage, the following provisions shall be in effect:

1.   The Promoter shall furnish to the Company's agent not later than ten days before the scheduled date of the engagement a ticket manifest of the facility setting forth the number of tickets available in each price category. All tickets shall be sold in accordance with such manifest. The Company will have the right to approve all ticket prices.

2.   It is agreed that the Agreement is computed on the basis of estimates for total expenses received by the Company from the Promoter. A list of these estimated expenses is attached hereto (Exhibit A), and no increase to these expenses will be allowed without the written approval of the Company.

3.   The Promoter will provide the Company's tour manager or his/her representative with a copy of the certified ticket manifest and a list of all show expenses actually incurred immediately prior to opening the box office on the day of the engagement. In a case in which ticket prices vary according to whether they are purchased on the day of the engagement or before, the Promoter will obtain different colored tickets for each type and price of sale. The Promoter will present to the representative of the Company a signed statement of the number and prices of all tickets sold in advance (prior to the opening of the box office on the day of the engagement), together with all of the unsold pre–show day tickets.

4.   The Company's tour manager shall have the right to check numbers of admissions and box office receipts at any time during or prior to the performance. The Promoter must produce all unsold tickets and a certified printer's manifest at the end of the engagement for the tour manager's (or his/her representative's) inspection. All other tickets, except for those produced at the end of the engagement intact, shall be deemed to have been sold, and the Company shall receive payment at the highest ticket price in the venue accordingly.

5.   All counterfeit tickets shall be the responsibility of the Promoter, and the Company shall receive the full percentage payment for any admissions that result from such counterfeit tickets. The Promoter shall provide a full written breakdown of the promotional costs (including advertising costs) with valid receipt for the tour manager's (or his/her representative's) inspection on the night of the engagement with a certified box office statement of the admissions, a photocopy of which and the breakdown of promotional costs must be sent to the Company's agent within seven days of the engagement.

6.   The Promoter warrants that all advance tickets will be available at list price and that if the Promoter has a booking office, the ticket for the engagement will not be subject to any booking fees.

7. The Company expects that the entire floor area in indoor shows be sold as general admission, standing only, and the Promoter must advise the Company at once if this is not the case.

8. A representative of the Company shall have the right to be present in the box office prior to, during, and after the performance.

9. Percentage payments provided for hereunder shall be accompanied by a written signed statement of box office receipts from the Promoter and shall be forwarded to the Company within three days of the engagement.

10. All drop stubs and unsold tickets shall be retained by the Promoter for ninety (90) days after the date of the engagement, during which time a representative of the Company shall be entitled to count and examine them and further the right to inspect the books and records of the Promoter so far as they relate to the engagement.

11. All percentage payments provided for herein shall be paid to the tour/business manager or representative of the Company prior to the performance.

   a) Percentage payments will be accompanied by a signed written statement from the Promoter, together with a certified invoice for each expense incurred by the Promoter in connection with the production of the engagement. All expenses will be compared with the estimated expenses previously furnished by the Promoter, and all expenses in excess of those shown prior to the date of the expense will not be included in the expenses for this performance and will be the Promoter's responsibility.

   b) If the actual aggregate paid expenses relating to any of the costs contained in Exhibit A hereto total less than estimated, then the expenses used to compute the percentage fee will be the actual costs as established to the reasonable satisfaction of the Company's tour manager (or his/her representative) based on the books, records, and paid bills maintained by the Promoter in connection with the performance.

12. If there is any assessment of tax by any taxing authority on the Company for moneys earned during the engagement, the said tax is to be paid by the Promoter. It must be understood and agreed that no deductions whatsoever are to be taken from the contract price contained herein or from any percentages earned hereunder.

13. Ticket prices and the number of tickets available in each price category must appear on the face of this contract. All tickets shall be printed by a bonded ticket printer or if the engagement is at a college or university, the official printing department of the college or university.

14. Any production fee as set out in the concert agreement shall be paid separately from and in addition to the performance fees set out in the concert agreement.

HALL AGREEMENT

1. The Promoter shall provide the Company with a copy of the Promoter's agreement with the hall and any additional documents relating to this engagement before the tickets are put on sale.

2. The Promoter may withhold from sale only the number of tickets set forth in his/her agreement with the hall. If the Promoter withholds any additional tickets for the hall, the Promoter shall be required to account for them as if they had been sold at the highest ticket price in the hall.

COMPLIMENTARY TICKETS

1. The Promoter will hold one hundred (100) complimentary tickets for use by the Company in locations requested by the Company. Should these not be used, they will be returned for sale to the public by 6:00 P.M. on the day of the performance, but no such tickets may be allotted from the first twenty rows.

2. Except as specifically provided above, the Promoter shall not distribute complimentary tickets nor permit the same to be distributed. The Promoter shall not, in any event, discount tickets as a premium, package, or series of concerts or performances or impose or permit to be imposed any service or handling charge on or in connection with the sale of tickets except and unless the Company shall grant prior express written permission, which it may refuse to do in its absolute discretion.

3. If people are admitted on the guest list, they shall not be entitled to enter with friends who are not named on the guest list.

4. The tour manager shall have the absolute approval of any "backstage list." Exhibit B will be the only authorized form for this use.

COUNTERFEIT TICKETS

The responsibility for the prevention of counterfeiting of tickets lies with the Promoter, and the Company shall not accept any loss in respect of such tickets.

MERCHANDISING

All rights to the band's merchandising rest with the Company, and the Company has licensed such rights to _____. The Company or its

GUEST LIST					
DATE:					
VENUE:					
NAME	GUEST OF	TICKETS	AFTERSHOW	V.I.P.	COLLECTED
	TOTAL				

Figure A1–1.   Exhibit B. Guest list.

designee will have its own merchandising crew at all performances, and the Promoter is requested to take all reasonable measures to ensure that these individuals are able to undertake the sale of the goods as advantageously as possible. If there is not an established concessionaire at the hall, the Promoter may not appoint one for this show. The Company or its representative will deal directly with the Promoter in connection with a fair site fee for the concession for this show.

If any support act wishes to sell its own merchandise in the venue, then notice of its wish to do so must be given to the Company at least seven days before the engagement or engagements.

The Promoter hereby undertakes to use its best endeavors to prevent or stop the illicit or unauthorized sale of the band's merchandise or any other merchandise (other than food and drink) inside or outside the venue.

PROMOTER'S EXPENSES, VERIFICATION, SETTLEMENT

The Promoter will present to the tour accountant at 3 P.M. on the day of the engagement originals of all bills, receipts, invoices, rental agreements, sponsorship agreements, advertising copy, staff time sheets, local tax and copyright laws, insurance documents, and related materials that prove the costs of this engagement. All must be originals (copies will be made at settlement) pertaining to this engagement, naming the band and dated.

These costs must be only out of pocket expenses by the Promoter and must be on a most favored nation basis with each supplier. The Promoter agrees to keep the costs to an absolute minimum in relation to similar events. All staff costs must be justified by signed receipts by the individual, his/her superior, and the venue manager; time sheets; and previous show documents. All print advertising must have the detailed invoice, each individual dated tear sheet, and a signed affidavit (with the signee's telephone number) from the publication manager confirming the rate charged and insertion details. All radio advertising must have a detailed invoice backed up by a signed affidavit from the station manager (with his/her telephone number) and a cassette tape of the spot. All expense items submitted must be net of any commissions to any party whatsoever. Any long-term venue rental agreement, related rates and cutoff conditions, and purchaser interests or shares in supplier companies or ticket agencies that add a booking fee must be revealed at this time. The final box office statement must be signed by the box office manager, the venue manager, and the Promoter. The tour accountant will use the documents to determine the percentage break figure, but the figure will be no higher than stated on the face of this contract. No damage deposits will be allowed as expenses. All expenses that are not properly verified shall not be included and will be the sole responsibility and liability of the Promoter.

Settlement Schedule

10:00 A.M.

House seating plan

Printer's manifest

Box office sales printout at 1 P.M.

Documents for advertising

Production

Catering

Insurance

Local tax laws

Local copyright laws

Hall rental

Staff proposed time sheets

Sponsorships and any other relevant documents

4:00 P.M.

Stubs of all sold tickets

All tickets available for sale

Vouchers for ticket exchanges

Comp list with seat numbers

Comp list for tonight

9:00 P.M.

Box office final statement

Comp lists plus uncollected tickets plus passes; ticket drop in packs of one hundred tickets

Deadwood (tickets that are unsold)

11:00 P.M.

Final staff documents

CONTRACT RIDER

[The following contract rider illustrates some of the requirements a show and its company may have.]

STAGING

With the exception of personnel directly involved with the running of the show who will be issued passes, the stage and the immediate surrounding area will be cleared completely during the performance. During the entire performance, the stage area will be under the absolute supervision of the Company's production manager. The security guards must be informed that only those people with passes may be admitted to the stage area.

The Promoter shall furnish at his/her sole cost and expense the stage in accordance with the plans. These plans must be followed exactly as to every detail.

If the Promoter has any difficulties or questions arising from the plans, then he/she must immediately contact the production manager.

The show will not take place unless the stage is set up in accordance with the plans.

Please note that the stage, that is, back wall, cycle track, fire exits, and so on, must be totally level and clear of all obstructions by a minimum of eight (8) feet.

MIXING POSITIONS

Both sound and lighting mixers shall be placed at stage center thirty (30) meters back. The sound mixer shall be on a platform five (5) meters wide and five (5) meters deep and half (0.5) a meter high. The final placing of this sound mixer must be approved by the Company's production manager. The lighting mixer will be on a platform four (4) meters wide, four (4) meters deep, and one (1) meter high. The position and size of these platforms are subject to change, and the Promoter will be given final measurements and positions by the production manager.

SPOTLIGHTS

The Promoter must provide five (5) suitable and adequate front of house (FOH) spotlight support towers or at the request of the production manager, five (5) suitable, sturdy, and secure positions for the front of house (FOH) spotlights. The position of the spotlights and the type of spotlight supports will be decided by the production manager, and he/she will inform the Promoter in good time. In addition, there will be four (4) spotlights and operators in the lighting truss.

The Promoter will bear the wages of the nine (9) spotlight operators on a per spotlight per show basis.

FORKLIFTS

The Promoter must provide one (1) forklift in good working order, which must have a capacity to lift two (2) tons and extend five (5) meters. If the production manager reasonably considers that access to the hall is difficult, he/she can call for additional handling equipment, which the Promoter will supply at his/her sole cost. The Promoter must provide fuel for the entire working period, and a pair of extension forks of 1.25 meters must be available for use.

POWER REQUIREMENTS

Power will be required for lights, Vari-lites, sound, rigging, and catering. The exact power requirements will be advised by the production manager as soon as possible.

PIANO TUNER

The Promoter must provide an experienced, competent piano tuner at a time to be requested by the production manager on the day of the engagement.

RIGGING

The stage lights and sound are designed primarily to be flown. If there are no satisfactory flying points in the hall, then the Promoter must inform the tour manager upon receipt of this rider. The Company will provide a ground support system for the stage lights if required, and this will be regarded as an additional cost.

The area in front of the stage is to be kept clear of all obstructions at all times. There should be no chairs between the front edge of the stage and the front of the mixing desk during the load in. The production manager will advise the Promoter when chairs can be placed in this area. The Promoter must provide a chair-striking crew to move the chairs before and after the show, and this crew must be separate from the production stagehands.

LOADING DOCK

There must be an adequate loading area with clear and easy access to the stage. This area and all access points must be well lit at all times when loading or unloading is in progress.

WORK LIGHTS

The Promoter must ensure that the venue has adequate work lights to provide a safe working environment for the Company's personnel in all parts of the venue. In addition, all access points, stairways, parking areas, and the route from the artists' dressing rooms to the stage must be clean and clear of all obstructions and well lit at all times.

CREW

Under normal conditions, the Promoter must provide a labor force of forty (40) stagehands who must be available from load in time until the show has been broken down and loaded back into the trucks. These stagehands must be fit, sober, older than eighteen (18) years, and prepared to take orders and instructions from the production manager or his/her representatives. All stagehands must be fed and available to work at the call times set by the production manager. The Promoter acknowledges that the number of stagehands required during the engagement will vary, and the production manager or his/her representative will be responsible for coordinating the use of the stagehands.

The Promoter must supply two (2) English-speaking runners who must be fluent in English and the language of the country in which the show takes place. Each runner must be able to drive and have a full valid driving license and any other certification needed to drive in the relevant country. One of the runners must drive a cargo van, and one of them must drive a four-seater car. The drivers are to be under the direction and control of the production manager and must only be used for reasons authorized by him/her. In addition, the Company's caterers will require one (1) person to help with washing up and kitchen duties.

GENERAL SECURITY

The Promoter shall provide adequate, clearly identifiable, and responsible security staff from the time of the load in until all the equipment has been fully loaded in the vehicles at the end of the show, for the protection of the band's equipment both on and off stage. General hall security personnel will be expected to wear the uniform normally worn, but any security personnel positioned behind the crowd control barricades must wear black T-shirts.

Within this general stipulation, the Promoter shall, in particular, provide the following personnel:

1. Four (4) persons to be available from the time the band arrives at 4:00 P.M.
2. From 6:00 P.M. or from the time the doors open, whichever shall be sooner, one (1) person per access point to the backstage area at all times.
3. One (1) person for the dressing rooms.
4. Two (2) persons, one (1) on each side of the stage behind the public address system.
5. Two (2) persons at the house mix position in the auditorium.
6. After the performance at least four (4) additional persons to assist in the backstage area to control all visitors, autograph hunters, and so on.
7. Three (3) security persons and one (1) guard dog to guard the buses and trucks.
8. One (1) person at each house spotlight position.

At all times from the arrival of the equipment, the security personnel must take their instructions from the tour manager or whomever he/she delegates for this job. This particularly applies to security staff backstage, onstage, and front of stage. Before the doors open, the tour manager or his/her delegate must be introduced to the person in charge of security, who must speak fluent English and take his/her instructions from the tour manager. The Promoter will arrange a meeting between the tour manager or his/her delegate and all security staff before the doors are open. A sign-in sheet will be mandatory for all personnel. In the event of unreasonable violence by any security personnel upon members of the public, the Company reserves the right to cancel or terminate the show immediately, and the Company will be entitled to its full contracted fee.

The Promoter must not permit anyone backstage who does not have a pass issued by the tour manager or his/her delegate. The Promoter agrees that any passes issued by the Company will be recognized by the security personnel. The tour manager will show the Promoter's representative all types of passes that the Company has issued. Passes issued by the Promoter will not be valid.

BARRICADES

The Company will provide its own front of stage barricades, running the length of the stage and the public address system. The Promoter will inform the production manager at once if he/she believes this will cause any problems with the local authorities.

HALL SECURITY

The Promoter shall provide an adequate security staff of experienced, properly trained, unarmed, and nonuniformed personnel who will work in connection with the tour manager or his/her delegate.

Where there are seats in the hall, patrons should be allowed to stand up in front of their seats during the performance, and the hall manager must not take it upon himself/herself, nor will the security personnel take it upon themselves, to ask people to sit down in their seats. However, the Company expects security personnel to make every effort to keep fire aisles clear until the show's finale.

BACKSTAGE SECURITY

The Company shall provide administrative, technical, and security personnel with badges that must be worn to enable them to gain access to the area where the public will not be admitted. No persons without passes (which must be worn) may be admitted to the backstage area, and on the day of each performance, no personnel whatsoever will be admitted to the dressing rooms of the band without their express approval. This includes facility personnel.

EQUIPMENT SECURITY

Five (5) security guards and two (2) trained guard dogs are required overnight on any consecutive engagement. The positions of the guards and dogs will be advised by the production manager, and if required, the guards must work in shifts. These guards should be available for assignment immediately after the show and must remain on duty or on working shifts until crew and show security personnel return the following day.

CATERING

Dressing Rooms

The following items are to be ready upon arrival (approximately 4:00 P.M., time to be confirmed by artist's production manager). There should be a plentiful supply of condiments, silverware, napkins, cups for hot beverages, and sixteen-ounce (16 oz.) colored cups for all dressing rooms.

MAIN DRESSING ROOM

The following requirements must accommodate four or more (4+) people.

- Hot, fresh coffee, not decaffeinated (please provide one [1] pound of freshly ground coffee purchased from a local specialty store)
- Hot water for tea and herbal decaffeinated teas
- Half and half (no milk or cream substitutes), sugar, and honey
- One (1) gallon freshly squeezed orange juice (not orange drink)
- Six (6) one-liter (1 L) bottles of spring water on ice (any substitutes for spring water must be uncarbonated and approved by production or tour manager)
- One (1) six-pack of 7-Up or Sprite
- One (1) six-pack of ginger ale
- Six (6) cans of assorted sodas on ice
- Sandwich ingredients: Swiss cheese, tomatoes, lettuce, avocado (whenever possible), mustard, and mayonnaise. *Don't forget the bread* (white and wheat).
- Fresh fruits (pineapples, seedless grapes, and strawberries are appreciated wherever possible in addition to other fruits)
- A cutting board and knife
- Peanut chocolate candies
- Adequate clean ice for drinks

BAND DRESSING ROOM

The following requirements must accommodate six or more (6+) people.

- Hot, fresh coffee, not decaffeinated
- Herbal decaffeinated teas
- Twelve (12) large bottles of spring water
- One (1) gallon of milk
- One (1) gallon of freshly squeezed orange juice
- One-half gallon of apple juice
- Assortment of Dole juices (Raspberry Passion, Tropical Breeze, Papaya) (mix of small and large bottles)
- Green Gatorade

- Beer on ice
  Twelve (12) bottles of light beer
  Twelve (12) bottles of domestic amber beer
  Six (6) bottles of nonalcoholic beer
- Wine
  Two (2) bottles of chardonnay or sauvignon blanc
  One (1) bottle of Chianti classico
- Sandwich ingredients (enough for ten [10] sandwiches), including avocado, tomatoes, lettuce, Swiss cheese, Monterey Jack cheese, sprouts, roasted breast of turkey, wheat bread, mayonnaise, Dijon or Grey Poupon mustard
- Whole fresh fruits, especially bananas (lots), grapes, oranges, apples, pears, raisins (in small boxes), melons, and berries (in season)
- Two (2) bags of tortilla chips
- One dozen (12) Tiger Milk bars
- Rice cakes
- Granola and assorted boxes of cereals
- Assortment of oat, bran, and blueberry muffins
- Assorted candies: chocolate plain and peanut candies, peanut butter cups (miniatures)
- Cashew nuts
- Adequate clean ice for drinks

BACKGROUND SINGERS' DRESSING ROOM
The following requirements must accommodate four or more (4+) people.

- Hot vegetable soup
- Two (2) pots of hot water and assorted herbal teas, honey, and lemons
- Small individual bottles of juice
- Six (6) bottles of spring water
- Croissants
- Small deli tray for sandwiches: wheat bread, turkey, roast beef, tomatoes, sprouts, Swiss cheese, avocado, lettuce, sandwich spreads—*no onions, they stink!*
- Wine
  One (1) bottle chardonnay
  One (1) bottle fumé blanc
- Whole fruit, including bananas

CHOIR ROOMS

- Two (2) cases of assorted sodas on ice
- Bottled spring water

Performance Area before Show

The following items should be iced down in a container placed at stage left no later than 7:30 P.M.

Five (5) large bottles of spring water

Six (6) bottles of beer, specifically Beck's, Heineken, Corona, or Samuel Adams brands

Two (2) bottles of light beer

One-half (1/2) gallon of apple juice

Three (3) cans of soft drinks (e.g., Coke, Sprite)

A supply of sixteen-ounce (16-oz.) Solo cups

Meals

The following setup is required at a time to be advised by the artist's production manager.

BREAKFAST

A hot-cooked breakfast for artist's crew is to be ready upon arrival, that is, thirty (30) minutes before load in. Also provide the following:

- Two (2) sixty-four–ounce (64-oz.) cartons of freshly squeezed orange juice
- Two (2) sixty-four–ounce (64-oz.) cartons of assorted fresh juices
- An ample supply of fresh milk, both regular and skim
- One (1) case assorted sodas
- One (1) case of one-liter (1 L) bottles of spring water
- Three (3) one-liter (1 L) bottles of carbonated water
- One (1) one-gallon (1 gallon) jug of spring water
- Hot, fresh coffee (regular and decaffeinated)
- Hot water for tea
- Cereals and pastries
- Toast and English muffins
- Mixed jellies and preserves, honey, and related condiments
- Fresh whole fruits

There should be a plentiful supply of condiments, silverware, napkins, hot-beverage cups, and sixteen-ounce (16-oz.) Solo cups.

LUNCH

Lunch will be served at approximately 12:00 P.M. There should be enough for all workers. The menu should consist of the following:

- Soup and salad
- Hot sandwiches

- Fresh fruit
- Two (2) cases of assorted sodas
- Two (2) gallons of whole and skim milk
- One (1) case of one-liter (1 L) bottles of spring water
- One (1) case of one-liter (1 L) bottles of carbonated water
- An ample supply of spring water
- Hot, fresh coffee
- Hot water for tea
- All necessary condiments, silverware, napkins, hot cups, and sixteen-ounce (16-oz.) colored Solo cups

DINNER

At 5:30 P.M. for ninety (90) people. This number includes artist, artist's band, artist's crew, choir, and support act only—it does not include local stage crew. Because of the number of vegetarians in the group, a two (2) entree dinner is usually the easiest to please all. Dinner should include the following:

- Salad—a wide variety of fresh vegetables, at least three (3) salad dressings
- Fresh cooked vegetables—steamed or stir fried in vegetarian oils
- Potatoes or whole-grain brown rice
- Dessert—no white flour, sugar, or preservatives
- Ample supply of spring water
- Ample supply of milk, regular and skim
- One (1) case of one-liter (1 L) bottles of carbonated water
- Hot, fresh coffee
- Hot water for tea
- Mixed sodas

Local specialties are welcome when cleared with the production manager or tour manager in advance. In addition to the catering provided by Promoter, menus from the finest local Italian, Chinese, Mediterranean, Indian, Japanese, Thai, and other suitable restaurants would be appreciated. In addition to the following list, a vegetarian entree and meatless pasta entree must be provided each day.

Monday
Roast beef

Roast turkey

Tuesday
Steak

Roast chicken

Fish

Baked potatoes recommended

Wednesday
Italian food—several meat and meatless pasta dishes

Several varieties of pizza, including cheese, vegetarian, and pepperoni

Thursday
Roast beef

Roast chicken

Vegetarian lasagna

Friday
Barbecue night—steak, chicken, and ribs

Saturday
Beef stroganoff

Fried chicken

Sunday
Chinese food—stir fried vegetables, fried rice, white rice, and a variety of other Chinese dishes

The artist travels with his own chef. The chef must be able to prepare a meal the day of the show in the venue close to the dressing room. If the use of propane fuel is prohibited inside the venue, then electric cooking equipment must be made available.

AFTER-SHOW CREW BUSES

The following are required for three buses. All quantities listed are per bus.

- Thirty (30) pounds of ice
- Two (2) cases of imported beer
- One (1) case of spring water
- One (1) case of assorted juices, including cranberry
- One-half (1/2) case of Coca-Cola or Pepsi-cola, one-half (1/2) case of ginger ale, one-half (1/2) case of Sprite or 7-Up
- One (1) six-pack of nonalcoholic beer
- One (1) gallon of apple juice

- Food for twelve (12) people to be advised day of show with necessary utensils, plates, and cups
- Cereals and one-half (1/2) gallon milk
- One package of chocolate chip cookies

After-Show Band Buses

First Band Bus
- Thirty (30) pounds of ice
- One (1) six-pack imported beer
- Two (2) six-packs light beer
- Twelve (12) bottles spring water
- Twelve (12) bottles cranberry juice
- Two (2) one-half (1/2) gallon containers freshly squeezed orange juice
- Food for ten (10) people to be advised day of show with necessary utensils, plates, and cups
- One-half (1/2) gallon milk

Second Band Bus
- Thirty (30) pounds of ice
- Twelve (12) bottles spring water
- Twelve (12) bottles of juice (individual size)
- Two (2) one-half (1/2) gallon containers freshly squeezed orange juice
- One-half (1/2) gallon milk

DRESSING ROOMS

The windows of all dressing rooms should be sufficiently curtained to prevent viewing from the outside, and all windows must be secure. All rooms should be fitted with locks, and the keys must be given to the production manager on his/her arrival and held in his/her possession throughout his/her stay at the venue.

Main Band

The room is to be team size and equipped with one (1) full-length mirror, one (1) large, well-lit makeup mirror, tables, twelve (12) upholstered chairs, two (2) sofas, a coffee table, and a color television. There should be three (3) working electrical outlets and adjacent toilet facilities, showers, and tuning room. The following items are required: twenty-four (24) bath-size towels, ten (10) stage towels (per show day), six (6) bars of top-quality soap, two (2) boxes of tissues, ashtrays, two (2) large, empty trash cans, a steam iron, and an ironing board.

Band

A large dressing room is required suitable for three (3) female artists. The room should be equipped with one (1) full-length mirror, one (1) large, well-lit makeup mirror, two (2) tables, six (6) upholstered chairs, a sofa, and a coffee table. There should be three working electrical outlets and adjacent toilet and shower facilities. The following items are required: six (6) bath-size towels, six (6) stage towels (per show day), three (3) bars of top-quality soap, a box of tissues, ashtrays, a large, empty trash can, a steam iron, and an ironing board. This room should be as close as possible to the main band dressing room.

Wardrobe

A team-size room is required for use as the wardrobe room. It should contain three (3) working electrical outlets, one (1) full-length mirror, a table, and two (2) chairs.

Crew

A team-size room equipped with one (1) full-length mirror, tables, and twelve (12) upholstered chairs is required. There should be three working electrical outlets and adjacent toilet facilities. Seventy-two (72) large-size towels are to be available to the production manager on his/her arrival with twelve (12) bars of top-quality soap, one (1) large, empty trash can, and one (1) box of tissues.

Support Act

The room should be team size and equipped with a mirror, tables, and eight (8) chairs. There should be one (1) working electrical outlet, toilet facilities, ten (10) towels, and soap. This area must be separate from the area of the Company's dressing rooms.

Production

One room must be equipped with two (2) direct-dial telephones and one (1) fax line for use by the Company's staff. There should be one (1) trestle table, two (2) chairs, and three (3) working electrical outlets. The numbers of the telephones and the fax number must be confirmed to the Company's office as soon as possible but no later than three (3) weeks prior to show date. Location should be near the dressing rooms but separate from the Promoter's office. Another room, adjacent to the production room, must be provided for the management. This room must be equipped with a telephone with direct outside access, one (1) table, three (3) chairs, and three (3) electrical outlets. The cost of the telephones and fax in both rooms will be a production cost.

One (1) security guard is required for both rooms from 4:00 P.M. to midnight. All rooms with keys must be ready for occupation no later than 8:00 A.M. on the day of the performance. The Promoter shall ensure that these rooms are clean and are for the exclusive private use of the Company's staff and crew. An appropriate temperature level must be maintained in these rooms. These rooms must be in the same building as the auditorium and must be accessible to the stage without passage through the audience area.

The Promoter shall choose a well-run, efficient, fast laundry and dry cleaning establishment and advise that establishment that its services will be required on a same-day basis to serve the Company's requirements.

SOUND AND LIGHT REHEARSALS

The Promoter must ensure that all parties and unions involved in the preparation of the show are aware that there will always be a technical rehearsal and band sound checks on the day of the performance. These rehearsals and sound checks may take place at any time and will last as long as necessary. Any scheduled rest periods must take account of the need to have an uninterrupted rehearsal and sound check. The house electrician must be present in the hall during the entire time from load in until the completion of the load out.

The Promoter and hall security must ensure that no audience members are present during the technical rehearsal or band sound check.

The production manager must have complete control of the performance and sound check. Under no circumstances must the venue doors be opened for admission of the audience until the Promoter has been told to do so by the production manager or his/her delegate.

PARKING AND LOADING

The Promoter must make available sufficient secure parking within the boundaries of the venue (or, with the prior written approval of the tour manager, very close to the venue) to accommodate eight (8) sixty-foot (60 ft) tractor-trailer units and four (4) forty-five–foot (45 ft) buses. The buses must be parked as close as possible to the back of stage door and within twenty (20) feet of four (4) separate thirty-ampere (30 amp) two hundred-forty–volt (240 V) shorelines. If there is lying snow or ice in the parking area, then suitable actions should be taken to clear it from the parking area before the vehicles arrive. The parking and loading areas must be cleared of all vehicles and equipment during the load in and load out times and all equipment must be cleared from the backstage areas.

The backstage area and stage area must be kept clear of garbage at all times, and the Promoter must ensure that strenuous efforts are made to keep these areas clean.

All necessary parking permits must be obtained by the Promoter and be available for use well in advance of the arrival of the transport.

MEDICAL

A doctor with privileges of admission to a nearby hospital or clinic should be available on an emergency basis during all periods of construction, setup, performance, and tear down. The name and telephone number should be given to the Company's production manager or site coordinator. A throat specialist also should be available on an emergency call basis throughout the show days.

LOCAL TRANSPORT

The Promoter will provide four (4) stretch limousines with licensed chauffeurs who speak fluent English. These limousines should be able to ferry the band at the tour manager's reasonable request, and the tour manager or his/her delegate shall notify the Promoter of the exact times that the vehicles will be needed. The Promoter must also provide a luggage van with a competent English-speaking driver. It also may be necessary for the Promoter to provide a cargo van or other vehicle for the use of the band, in which case the tour manager or his/her delegate will notify the Promoter so that arrangements can be made.

COST AMENDMENT FORM

If the Promoter or the Company wishes to make a change to the rider that changes the costing in any way, then he/she shall use the following form. No changes will be accepted unless they are set down in this form and signed by both parties.

COST AMENDMENT FORM

DATE _____ VENUE _____

PROMOTER _____

CHANGE REQUESTED BY _____

CHANGE APPROVED BY _____

NATURE OF CHANGE (CIRCLE)

CATERING   STAGING   DRESSING ROOMS   SUPPLIES

MATERIALS   PARKING/LOADING   OTHER

EXPLANATION_____

This form is to be completed for all changes, additions, or deletions that affect cost and must be sent to the tour manager. Approval may be given only by the Company or the tour manager. Once signed approval has been given, the Promoter must give the original to the tour manager, keep one copy for himself/herself or his/her representative for use at the settlement, and send one copy to the Company.

INSURANCE

It is the essence of this Agreement that the Promoter will provide public liability insurance coverage against injuries to person or property as a consequence of the installation and/or operation of the equipment provided by the Company. Further, the Promoter shall maintain in effect a policy of employer's liability insurance or its equivalent in the relevant country covering all of its employees who are involved in the installation, operation, and/or maintenance of the equipment provided by the Company. The Promoter shall deliver to the Company by mail or fax a Certificate of Insurance showing above coverage at least two (2) weeks prior to the performance date.

The Promoter shall further indemnify and hold the Company, its contractors, employees, licensees, and assignees harmless from and against any loss damage, or expense, including reasonable attorney's fees incurred or suffered by, or threatened against the Company in connection with or as a result of any claim for personal injury or property damage or otherwise brought by or on behalf of any third-party person, firm, or corporation as a result of or in connection with the engagement, which claim does not result directly from the Company's, its employees', contractors', or agents' active negligence. To this end the Promoter will obtain at its sole expense a policy of insurance therefore naming the Company and the artists as additionally insured.

The Company may decide to take out nonappearance coverage for each performance, in which case the Promoter and his/her contractors will be named as an interested party and will pay an amount toward the premium to be notified to him/her by the tour manager at least seven (7) days before the engagement.

All employees of the Company and its subcontractors are covered by employer's liability insurance, and a copy of the certificate will be carried by the tour manager.

GENERAL RESTRICTIONS

The Company, either by itself or its licensees, shall have the exclusive right to sell and advertise for sale any items of merchandise whatsoever other than food or drink.

No sales of any sort may be permitted in the auditorium during the band's performance, and the lights on or in any vending concession in the auditorium must be switched off. The Promoter hereby undertakes to inform the vending concessionaires of these requirements in writing.

There shall be no advertising arranged by the Promoters on any tickets, programs, handbills, or posters, nor shall there be any advertising of any sort in the auditorium after 4:00 P.M. on the day of the show. The Promoter must not represent that the show is copromoted or sponsored by any third party whatsoever.

The Promoter must not commit the band to any interviews, personal appearances, or any other sort of promotional activity.

The Promoter acknowledges that the band's live performance is a unique work of art of great value and all rights in such performance are reserved exclusively to the Company. The Promoter will use his/her best endeavors to prevent any person entering the auditorium with audio or visual recording equipment. If any person is seen in the auditorium with such equipment during the performance, he or she must be ejected and the equipment confiscated until the end of the performance. The Promoter will post notices in prominent positions at all public entrances to the auditorium informing the public that recording devices are not allowed in the auditorium and that those who take them in may be ejected.

The Promoter must provide a safe place for any confiscated equipment to be held and must give each person whose equipment is confiscated a receipt to enable him or her to recover the equipment after the performance. Standard nonprofessional cameras may be taken into the auditorium.

If a visual or audio performance of the band made under this agreement is recorded and released in any commercial form, then the Promoter will immediately pay to the Company a stipulated fee by way of liquidated damages in addition to any other right the Company may have.

APPLICABLE LAW AND WARRANTIES

This Agreement constitutes the full binding agreement between the parties. No alteration may be made to any part of this agreement without prior written permission from the Company. Alterations or amendments will be accepted only when confirmed in writing by the Company.

The headings shown on the Agreement are for guidance only and have no legal significance.

If the Promoter shall commit a material breach of this Agreement, then the Company shall be entitled to terminate this Agreement immediately without prejudice to any other rights it may have under the Agreement. If such a breech occurs less than seven (7) days before the date of the performance, then the whole of the deposit paid by the Promoter shall be forfeit to the Promoter as immediate liquidated damages without prejudice to any other rights it may have. If such occurs on the day of the performance, then the whole of the guaranteed fee shall be forfeit to the Promoter as immediate liquidated damages without prejudice to any other rights it may have.

This Agreement will become binding upon the Company only when, after the Company has received an unamended copy signed by the Promoter, a copy signed on behalf of the Company is delivered to the Promoter.

PRODUCTION CHECKLISTS AND FORMS

The production checklists will help avoid any problems associated with presenting a show. With a checklist, one can identify most problems and arrange for suitable alternatives before the show. Always call ahead and check each detail to ensure a coordinated and smooth procedure. The forms can be customized for each tour.

The following is a hypothetical checklist for a tour with an indoor performance requiring two semitrailers and nine touring crew members. Each show's requirements differ.

Day: Wednesday
Date: 10/6/98
City: Anytown
Venue: Apollo
Address: 879 Desert Highway
Phone number: 418–267–3521

Show Times
Sound check: 4:30 P.M.
Doors open: 7:00 P.M.
Opening act: 8:00 P.M.
Changeover: 8:40 P.M.
Show time: 9:10 P.M.

Call Times
Rigging: 8:00 A.M.

Lighting: 9:00 A.M.

Sound: 10:00 A.M.

Set: 11:00 A.M.

Band equipment: 12.00 P.M.

Contacts
Venue technical manager: Bert Smith

Promoter's representative: Harry Jones

Opening act contact: Steve Normal

Security: Peter Muscle

Catering: Sharon Lunch

Venue Description
Capacity: 4720

Shape: Proscenium hall

Construction material: Concrete/steel

Age of building: 18 years

Highest seat: 32 feet above stage

Fire law restrictions: Control cables must be placed in duct

Proscenium width: 54 feet

Air conditioning: Exhaust system

Pyrotechnics restrictions: Fire marshal must be in attendance

Load In
Access: Loading dock at rear of stage

Clearance: 9 feet, 6 inches

Distance to stage: 25 feet

Difficulties: None

Loading lights: Yes

Parking
Trucks: Two trucks on dock

Cars: 20 spaces

Buses: Near loading dock

Limousines: At stage door

Forklifts

Height capacity: 15 feet

Weight capacity: 2000 pounds

Fuel: Propane

Tires: Pneumatic

Stage

Size available: Fixed, 60 feet wide, 54 feet deep

Size of modules: N/A

Type: Wood

Stairs: N/A; level with dock and dressing rooms

Masking: Black front

Soundwings

Size available: 16 feet wide, 8 feet deep

Type: Side of stage

Barricade

Type: Fixed

Height: 4 feet

Distance from stage: 4 feet

Width: Full width of stage

Mixing Positions

Sound console: House center

Lighting console: House center

Other: N/A

Cable route to console: Through duct

Power

Service 1: 600 A, three phase

Service 2: 200 A, three phase

Service 3: 100 A, three phase

Rigging

Beam to floor: 47 feet

Beam to ceiling: 6 feet

Beam to beam, up- and downstage: 12 feet

Beam to beam, cross-stage: 8 feet (no central beam)

Weight limits: 20,000 pounds

Distance to stage: on stage left, 41 feet

Distance to stage: on stage right, 41 feet

Catwalks: Adjacent to beams

Spotlights
Number available: Four

Type: Zenon troupers

Intercom: Not suitable

Houselight Control
Type: Quartz

Control location: Stage left

Dimmable: Yes

Catering
Facilities available: Kitchen and dining room

Meal times: Breakfast 7:30 A.M., Lunch 1:00 P.M., Dinner 6:00 P.M.

Dressing Rooms
Performers: Two very large rooms with bathrooms

Opening act: One large room without bathroom

Tuning room: Adjacent to stage

Production office: Yes, off stage left

Other Facilities Available
Laundry: No

Photocopier: Yes, in booking office

Work lights: Yes

Drapes for acoustics: N/A

Drapes for masking: Yes

Ladders: 16 foot A frame, tallascope

Video: 2 screens / 3 cameras

Local Staff Required
No

Stagehands
Minimum call: 3 hours
Breaks required: After 4 hours
Call times and numbers: 8:00 A.M., eight hands

Loaders
Minimum call: 3 hours
Breaks required: After 4 hours
Call times and numbers: 8:00 A.M., four loaders

Follow Spot Operators
Minimum call: 3 hours
Call times and numbers: 7:30 P.M., four operators

Piano Tuner
Time required: 2:00 P.M.
Piano type: Electrical/acoustical CP70

Electrician
Time required to connect: 8:00 A.M.
Time required to disconnect: 1:00 P.M.

Riggers
Time required: 8:00 A.M.
Climbing: Two
Groundwork: One

Forklift Operator
Time required: N/A

Runner
Time required: 8:00 A.M. with vehicle

Overnight Security
Time required: N/A
Number of guards: N/A

Additional Outdoor Checklist
Generators
Power capacity

RUNNER'S SHEET					
DATE	ITEM REQUIRED	REQ BY	DEPARTMENT	GIVEN TO	RUNNER

Figure A3–1.   Runner's list.

Generator fuel

Scaffolding

Mixing tower

Roof

Tarpaulins

Plastic

Raincoats

Work lights

Power feed cable

Access to mix tower

Budget Items

Stage

Sound wings

Mixing platform

Barrier

Roof

Sound system

Lighting system

Equipment transport

Personnel transport

Follow spots

Follow spot operators

Stagehands

Loaders

Riggers

Forklifts

Forklift driver

Piano tuner

Electrician

Runner

Telephones

Risers

Weatherproofing

Fuel

Drapes for masking

Drapes for acoustic treatment

Dressing rooms

Generators

Generator fuel

Accommodation

Catering

Security

Crew

TECHNICAL SPECIFICATIONS

AUDIO REQUIREMENTS

Front of House (FOH) Speakers
16 × Meyer MSL4

4 × Meyer 650P sub-bass

6 × Meyer MSL 2

4 × Meyer UPA—2C

FOH Consoles
1 × Yamaha PM 4000—44 Mono and eight (8) stereo channels

1 × Yamaha PM 4000 or 3000—32 channels

FOH FX
2 × Yamaha SPX 990

FOH Inserts
10 × DBX 160X compressors

4 × Drawmer DS 201 gates

1 × Klark Technic DN725 stereo delay line

FOH Drive
5 × Meyer CP-10 parametric EQ (equalizer)

1 × Klark Technic DN 360

1 × Klark Technic DN 60 analyzer

4 × stereo input delay units

FOH Playback

1 × compact disc (CD) player

1 × digital audiotape (DAT) player

2 × Akai DR4 VR hard disc recorders with CO (changeover) box

MONITORS

Monitor Speakers

6 × Meyer UM wedges

4 × UPA—2C (on lift-up speaker stands)

5 × Yamaha MS-202 self-powered speakers

Monitor Inserts

3 × Klark Technic DN 360 EQ

Headphones

1 × Rane 6-way headphone amplifier

6 × headphones

3 × 12 meter headphone cable extensions

2 × 3 meter headphone cable extensions

MICROPHONES

Vocal Radio System

6 x Shure UHF radio handhelds (beta 87 heads)

9 × Shure UHF radio beltpacks (microphones supplied)

Both systems will need antenna distribution splitter

Orchestra

12 x Countryman "o" (omnidirectional) or Crown String bug microphones (with clips and pop shields)

9 × Sennheiser 421

6 × AKG 535

1 × Beyer M88

5 × Shure SM 57

10 × Shure SM 81

3 × Shure SM 91

2 × AKG 414

8 × Active DI (direct injection) box

Microphone Extras

6 × Latin percussion drum microphone clamps

8 × 1 meter 6.5 mm to 6.5 mm jack leads

6 × foam pop shields for handheld radio microphones

8 × two male to one female XLR Y splits

Spare clips and pop shields for string bugs

Batteries for radios (new batteries each show)

Multicore

61 multicore lines plus appropriate system and monitor

Microphone Stands

Refer to microphone input list

VIDEO

8 × Panasonic WV 5340 9-inch video monitors

2 × Panasonic WV CP 410A video cameras

1 × 30 meter BNC to BNC video cable

1 × 50 meter BNC to BNC video cable

3 × 20 meter BNC to BNC video cable

5 × 3 meter BNC to BNC video cable

2 × video distribution amps

AUDIO EXTRAS

3 × walkie talkies

Intercom—3 station

LIGHTING REQUIREMENTS

Lighting requirements are defined in Figures A4–1 through A4–8.

LIGHTING EQUIPMENT SPECIFICATIONS

	LIGHTING	*SCENIC*
CONTROL:	Vari*Lite Artisan Plus (SV 3.0)	JANDS EVENT 36 (SV 3.0)
M/CORE:	V*L Snakes	1 x 100metre DMX
RACKS:	V*L ACS Rack	1 x Series '2' COLOURSET RACK
	V*L MOD. Rack	(plus 1 spare)
	2 x DMX/VLD	
DIMMERS:	3 x 48 Way Digital dimmers (Total Dimmers = 144)	2 x 36 Way Digital dimmers (Total Dimmers = 72)
LAMPS:	80 x SILVER PAR 64's (16 x 4 Lamp Bars/8 Half Bars)	16 x Single PAR 64's (10 x SILVER, 4 x BLACK, 2 x STUBBIE BLACK)
	(60 x MFL,20 x NSP)	(2 x MFL,14 x VNSP)
	8 x CODA 1's	16 x Series '2' COLOURSET Par Scrollers
	2 x 1K CCT/SIL 30's c/w shutters	(plus 2 spares)
	6 x DESISTI Top CYC Units	
	6 x PALLAS 4 Groundrow	
FX:	4 x White Lightning STROBES	10 x rosco Mirror panels
	2 x DF-50 Foggers c/w fans	
MAINS:	LX = 1 x 300amp	WALLS = 2 x 32amp
DRAPES:	1 x 44' x 2' border	1 x 40' x 24' STARCLOTH {TMALW to supply}
	1 x 44' x 3' border	1 x 40' x 24' WHITE S/T CYC {TMALW to supply}
	2 x 12' x 30' legs	2 x 12' x 30' legs
RIGGING:	15 x 1 Ton - CM	4 x 1 Ton - CM
	15 x 8' sections (A type)...5 x SILVER/10 x BLACK + 2 x Hinges	(plus 1 spare)
	12 x 10' sections (J type-tri)...All SILVER	6 x 10' sections (J type-tri)
	2 x 8' sections (J type-tri)...All SILVER	8 x 8'sections (J type-tri)
	4 x 45 deg Cnrs + 2 x 90 deg Cnrs (J type-tri)....All SILVER	4 x 90 deg VERTICAL CNRS...All SILVER
F.O.H. SPOTS:	2 x 2K ZENON or equivalents	

gels for spots are #1 = L201, #2 = L206, #3 = L110, #4 = L118, #5 = L158, #6 = L170

Figure A4-1. Lighting equipment specifications.

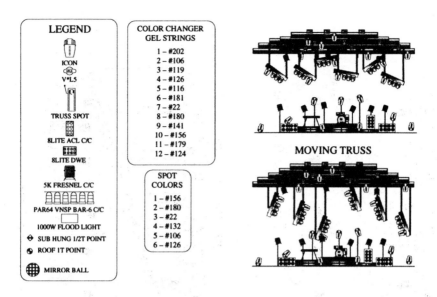

LEGEND

ICON

V*L5

TRUSS SPOT

8LITE ACL C/C

8LITE DWE

5K FRESNEL C/C

PAR64 VNSP BAR-6 C/C

1000W FLOOD LIGHT

◇ SUB HUNG 1/2T POINT

◎ ROOF 1T POINT

⊕ MIRROR BALL

COLOR CHANGER GEL STRINGS

1 – #202
2 – #106
3 – #119
4 – #126
5 – #116
6 – #181
7 – #22
8 – #180
9 – #141
10 – #156
11 – #179
12 – #124

SPOT COLORS

1 – #156
2 – #180
3 – #22
4 – #132
5 – #106
6 – #126

MOVING TRUSS

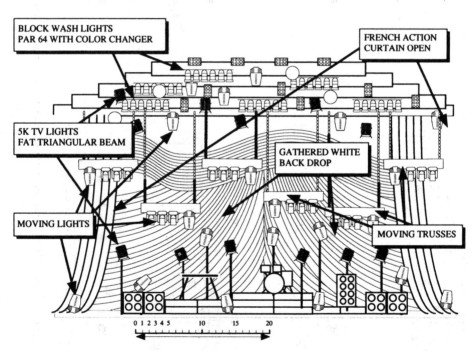

BLOCK WASH LIGHTS
PAR 64 WITH COLOR CHANGER

FRENCH ACTION
CURTAIN OPEN

5K TV LIGHTS
FAT TRIANGULAR BEAM

GATHERED WHITE
BACK DROP

MOVING LIGHTS

MOVING TRUSSES

0 1 2 3 4 5   10   15   20

Figure A4–2.   Lighting rig front view. Drawn and designed by Sean "Motley" Hackett.

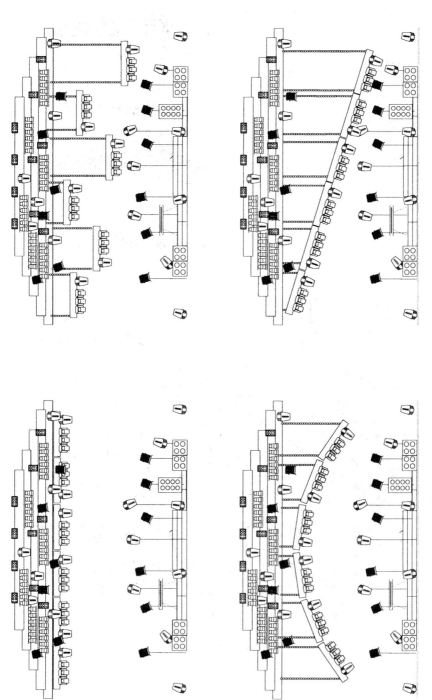

Figure A4–3. Different positions for subhung trusses. Drawn and designed by Sean "Motley" Hackett.

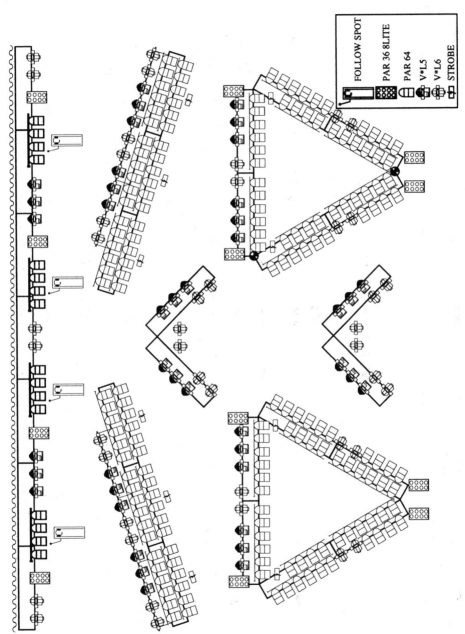

Figure A4-4. Rig lamp layout. Drawn and designed by Sean "Motley" Hackett.

FOLLOW SPOT

PAR 36 8LITE

PAR 64

V*L5

V*L6

STROBE

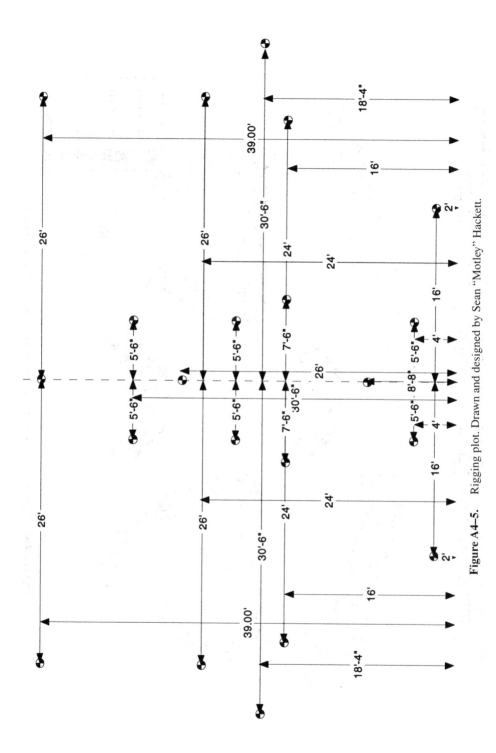

Figure A4-5. Rigging plot. Drawn and designed by Sean "Motley" Hackett.

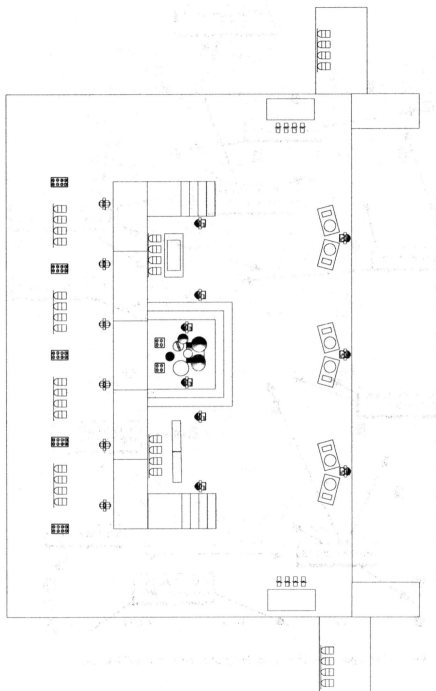

Figure A4–6. Floor lamp layout. Drawn and designed by Sean "Motley" Hackett.

89

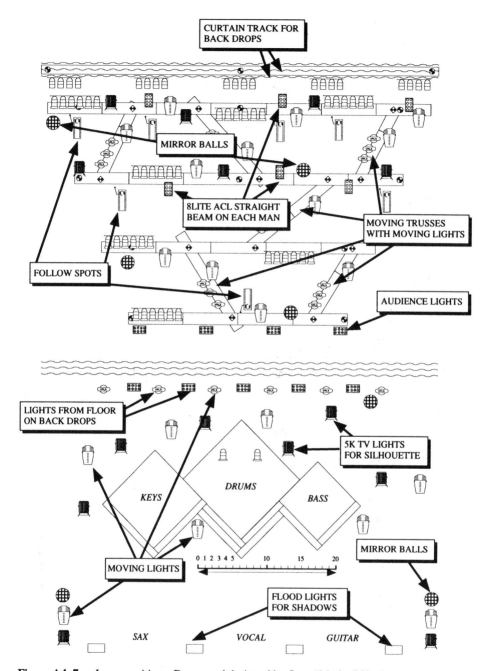

Figure A4–7. Lamp positions. Drawn and designed by Sean "Motley" Hackett.

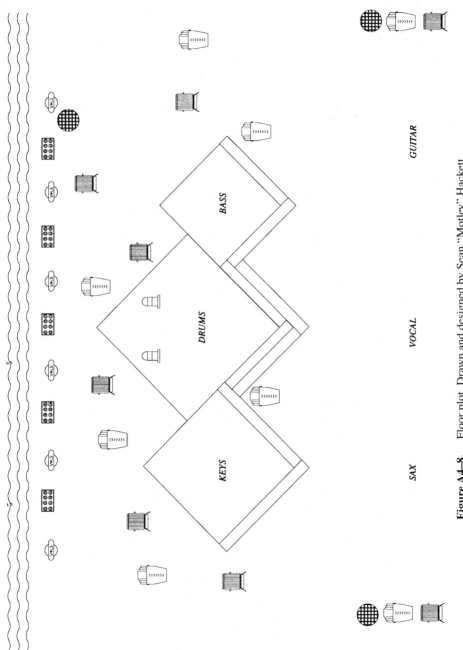

Figure A4–8. Floor plot. Drawn and designed by Sean "Motley" Hackett.

91

VENDOR CONTRACT

[The following is an example of the conditions that may accompany a quotation for sound and lighting services.]

This quote does not include the following: equipment transport, staff air travel and accommodation, staff ground travel, staff per diems ($?0.00 per day per person), loaders, stagehands, staging equipment, risers, sets, flooring, licensed riggers and electricians, weatherproofing, equipment insurance, power supply cables in excess of 22 meters from point of connection to supply (whether local authority mains, consumer subcircuits/mains, or generators), single-phase 110V/240V mains distribution and mains cable in addition to 15A, 240V, GPO (general purpose outlet) circuits supplied, locally booked equipment, venue equipment, production management, front of house (FOH) follow spots, forklifts, scaffolding, customs and carnet fees, operators for equipment, fog juice, additional gels, color change strings, and batteries.

Your acceptance of this quotation is subject to our terms and conditions.

Notwithstanding and without prejudice to said indemnity, the hire company reserves the right to refuse to connect and/or energize equipment it may deem to be unsuitable or unsafe. The hire company is completely indemnified in the event that equipment is connected to an electrical supply by means of bypassing the protection devices provided in the distribution system. Production services is further indemnified in the event of any mains equipment being operated by any persons other than production services staff or being other than under direct personal supervision of services staff.

It is a condition of your acceptance of this quotation that you shall agree to indemnify this company for all loss and/or damage in the event that such damage is caused as a result of any and all actions made by your company, your representatives, and/or partners, agents, and any or all third-party contractors or suppliers. Furthermore, we recommend that all contractors, riggers, staging, and roofing companies be required to hold full and comprehensive insurance, and it is in your best interest to have sight of such policies prior to commencement.

GOVERNING LAWS AND VENUE

The terms and conditions of this agreement shall be governed by the state in which this agreement is signed.

We look forward to receiving your written confirmation of your acceptance of this quotation and the liability condition as above prior to the commencement of providing services. By our commencement of providing services without your written objection to such action it shall be acknowledged that you accept the liability condition as laid out above.

VENUE CONTRACT

[The following is an example of a contract between a venue and a promoter. The production manager has to be aware of the conditions to which the promoter has agreed with the venue. The contract covers a great deal of legal obligations between both parties.]

HIRING AGREEMENT

Between:

_____

"The Licenser"
And:

_____

The party or parties more particularly described in Item 1 of Schedule 1 ("the Hirer")

TABLE OF CONTENTS

HIRING AGREEMENT

This agreement is made on the date specified on the signatory page of this agreement.

Between:

(hereinafter with its successors and assigns called "the Licenser")

And:

The party or parties more particularly described in Item 1 of Schedule 1 (hereinafter with its successors called "the Hirer")

Whereas:

A. The Licenser was appointed the manager and operator of the Entertainment Center pursuant to an agreement entitled and hereinafter referred to as "the Operating Agreement" between the City Council and itself on the 1st July 1995.

B. The management agreement provides, inter alia, that the Licenser shall conduct the business of the Center including making the Center available for the staging and performance of events.

C. The Hirer desires to stage the hiring (more particularly described in Item 2 of Schedule 1) at the Entertainment Center.

Now the parties hereby undertake and agree as follows:

1. DEFINITIONS AND INTERPRETATION

1.1

In this Agreement and the recitals and schedules hereto unless otherwise provided or unless there is something in the subject matter or context inconsistent therewith the expressions following shall have the meanings in this Clause 1 respectively assigned to them.

1.2

"Bookings Holding Account" means the account of the Licenser with a secure financial institution selected by the Licenser for the purposes of Clause 5.12.

1.3

"Box Office" means those outlets at which tickets for the Event are to be available for distribution pursuant to Clause 5.5.

1.4

"Business Day" means a day other than a weekend or a public holiday in the City of _____.

1.5

"The Center" means the building known as the Entertainment Center, together with the cartilage surrounding the building and such other areas as the Licenser and the Council shall, from time to time, agree are included in the expression "the Center" for the purposes of this Agreement.

1.6

"The Council" means the City Council.

1.7

"Event" means any individual performance, staging, exhibition, conference, meeting, tournament, banquet, function, trade show, or other event normally presented in a venue similar to the Center.

1.8

"Gross Box Office Receipts" means gross receipts from the sale of tickets for the Event inclusive of any fees or charges imposed in respect of the distribution of tickets by the Box Office (including, without limiting the generality of the foregoing all Box Office fees, booking fees, credit card fees, and telephone booking fees).

1.9

"Gross Box Office Proceeds" means the Gross Box Office Receipts less the aggregate of all fees or charges imposed in respect of the distribution of tickets by the Box Office (including, without limiting the generality of the foregoing, all Box Office fees, booking fees, credit card fees, and telephone booking fees) for any Event.

1.10

"The Hiring" means the agreed use of the License Area by the Hirer as specified in Item 2 of Schedule 1 and includes all events therein specified both in the aggregate and individually.

1.11

"The License" means the license granted by the Licenser to the Hirer pursuant to Clause 2.

1.12

"The License Area" means the area specified in Item 3 of Schedule 1, together with such other areas of the Center as the parties may agree, from time to time, to be part of the License Area.

1.13

"The License Period" means the period specified in Item 4 of Schedule 1.

1.14

"Management Agreement" is the term to define the conditions of management appointments.

1.15

"Patrons" means all persons who attend at or enter upon any part of the Center at any time during the Hiring.

1.16

"Principal Contractor" has the same meaning as the expression *principal contractor* in the Workplace Health and Safety Act of 1989 as amended from time to time.

1.17

"Security Deposit" means any amount deposited by the Hirer with the Licenser pursuant to Clause 3.2.

1.18

"Tickets" means instruments of admission or other rights of entry to any part of the Center for the purpose of viewing or participating in or otherwise in connection with the Event (as may be appropriate having regard to the nature of the Event).

1.19

"Workplace Health and Safety Act" means the Workplace Health and Safety Act of 1989 together with any amendments thereto and any regulations enacted pursuant to the said act.

1.20

"Writing" includes printed, typed, and other modes of reproducing words in a visible form, and "written" has a corresponding meaning.

1.21

Words denoting the singular number only will include the plural number and vice versa, words denoting a gender shall include both genders, and words denoting individual persons only will include corporations and vice versa.

1.22

The headings in this Agreement are included for convenience only and will not affect the construction of this Agreement.

1.23

To the extent that there exists any inconsistency between any provision in Clauses 1 through 12 of this Agreement and any provision in the Schedules, the provision in the Schedules shall prevail without affecting the interpretation of the remaining part of this Agreement.

1.24

The reference to Clauses (save where the context refers specifically to another instrument) will be references to Clauses in this Agreement.

1.25

References in this Agreement to another instrument or to this Agreement or to an act, bylaw, or regulation (save where there is something in the subject matter or context inconsistent therewith) shall be references to such instrument or this Agreement or act, bylaw, or regulation and all amendments, variations, and supplements thereto and hereto.

1.26

The schedules and annexures to this Agreement shall for the purposes hereof be deemed to form part of this Agreement.

2. Hiring of the Center

2.1 GRANT OF LICENSE

Subject to the provisions of this Agreement the Licenser grants to the Hirer license and authority to use the License Area during the License Period for the Hiring, and the Hirer agrees to undertake the Hiring accordingly. Notwithstanding references to the Center for particular purposes throughout this Agreement, the license and authority granted herein is strictly limited to the License Area, but the Hirer's responsibility will extend to all areas in any way used by the Hirer's servants, agents, invitees, and licensees.

2.2 LICENSE NOT EXCLUSIVE

The use of the License Area will not be exclusive, and possession of the Center will remain with the Licenser, and this Agreement shall not in any way create a tenancy between the Licenser and the Hirer.

2.3 HIRER IS PRINCIPAL CONTRACTOR

The Licenser on its own behalf and for and on behalf of the City Council hereby appoints the Hirer as Principal Contractor, and the Hirer accepts such appointment.

3. FEES AND PAYMENTS

3.1 LICENSE CHARGE

In consideration of the License hereby granted, the Hirer will pay to the Licenser the amounts on the dates and in the manner all as specified in Item 1, Part A of Schedule 2 ("Item 1 charges") and all amounts incurred in respect of any of the matters specified in Item 2, Part A of Schedule 2, as determined by the Licenser in good faith ("Item 2 charges"). In the event that a date for payment is not specified in Schedule 2 in respect of any item, payment shall be made immediately upon demand at the completion of the Event or otherwise if specifically permitted by the Licenser within seven (7) days of the date of invoice in respect of such item issued by the Licenser.

Notwithstanding anything contained in this Clause or in Schedule 2, Item 1 charges and Item 2 charges shall accrue daily and shall become due and payable at midnight on the day in respect of which the charge is incurred.

3.2 SECURITY DEPOSIT

3.2.1.   The Hirer will lodge with the Licenser on or before the date or dates specified in Part B of Schedule 2 the amount or amounts set out against the respective dates, or otherwise on the date of signing of this Agreement, as and by way of security for the due observance and performance by the Hirer of the conditions of this Agreement *provided however* that the Licenser may waive such deposit if in the opinion of the Licenser moneys held by or on behalf of the Licenser arising out of sales of tickets by the Licenser or its subagents are sufficient to cover amounts ultimately due to the Licenser hereunder.

3.2.2.   In the event that:

i.   In the opinion of the Licenser, the estimated Gross Box Office Proceeds for the Event may not exceed the total amount, the Hirer is liable to pay to the Licenser hereunder;

ii. In the opinion of the Licenser, the Hirer may not be in a position to pay the Licenser all moneys due and payable pursuant to the Hiring Agreement at the time required by the Hiring Agreement;

iii. In the opinion of the Licenser, the Event may not proceed on the dates nominated in the Hiring Agreement;

iv. In the opinion of the Licenser, circumstances may arise that require a refund to Patrons of moneys paid for a ticket or tickets to attend the Event; or

v.   In the opinion of the Licenser, the Hirer may not discharge its obligations to the Licenser under the Agreement, the Licenser may require the Hirer to deposit with the Licenser such further moneys or provide such further security as the Licenser may require.

3.2.3.   All such moneys or such further security as the Licenser requires shall be paid to or provided to the Licenser by the Hirer upon demand.

3.2.4.   A failure by the Hirer to comply with Clause 3.2.3 herein shall constitute a fundamental breach of the Agreement, and the Licenser may, upon noncompliance with Clause 3.2.3, at its option, terminate the Agreement without prejudice to any rights vested in the Licenser under the Agreement.

3.3 HIRER CHARGES RIGHT TO SECURITY DEPOSIT
The Hirer hereby charges all its rights, title, and interest in respect of any moneys deposited pursuant to Clause 3.2 in favor of the Licenser as security for all moneys due and payable by the Hirer to the Licenser from time to time under this Agreement.

3.4 LICENSER TO SET OFF SECURITY DEPOSIT
The Hirer hereby specifically authorizes the Licenser, at any time and from time to time, to deduct from and retain out of any Security Deposit held by the Licenser such amounts as it may think fit and to apply or set off such amounts in or toward or against satisfaction of any liability of the Hirer under this Agreement, including damages for breach of this Agreement.

3.5 LICENSER TO REPAY SECURITY DEPOSIT
Subject to Clause 3.4, provided the Hirer shall have complied in all respects with the terms and conditions of this Agreement and shall have discharged in full the whole of its liability to the Licenser under this Agreement the Licenser will, within 30 days following the completion of the Event, repay to the Hirer the whole of any such Security Deposit or such part thereof as shall remain after deduction of any amounts pursuant to Clause 3.4.

3.6 ADDITIONAL RENTALS FOR OVERRUNS
If the Hirer or any equipment associated with the Hiring continues to occupy the License Area beyond the License Period and, in the sole opinion of the Licenser, causes any inconvenience or disruption to the work of the Licenser, the Hirer will pay the Licenser by way of additional rental in respect of each 24-hour period or part thereof after the "time by which Hirer must be clear of Center at the end of License Period" as specified in Item 5 of Schedule 1, an additional amount equal to the average daily charge applicable to the Hiring as specified in Item 1 of Part A of Schedule 2, and the Hirer will further indemnify the Licenser against any claim against the Licenser by any other person inconvenienced through such overrun, and will also reimburse the

Licenser for any consequential loss occurring through such overrun. The remedies provided by this Subclause and Subclause 4.31 may both apply and are not mutually exclusive save that the Hirer shall not be obliged to pay additional rental by reason only of not having removed certain equipment from the License Area to the extent to which such equipment has been dealt with pursuant to Subclause 4.31.

3.7 STAMP DUTY

The Hirer will pay any stamp duty assessed on this Agreement, its copies, or any other instrument between the parties that is collateral to or incidental to this Agreement.

3.8 LEGAL COSTS

The Hirer will pay all legal costs and consultant's fees incurred by the Licenser in any way in respect to this Agreement, including any costs incurred by the Licenser with respect to any request by the Hirer for any variation from the terms of the Licenser's standard Hiring Agreement for the Center and for any actual variation and in any claim or action against the Hirer, or in giving notices to the Hirer or enforcing any terms of the Hiring Agreement or any other costs incurred in connection with any breach by the Hirer of this Agreement or in the performance or observance of any of the terms and conditions of this Agreement.

3.9 HIRER TO SATISFY ITSELF AS TO CHARGES

Prior to entering into this Agreement the Hirer will satisfy itself as to all charges which the Licenser is entitled to make hereunder. The Licenser will upon request inform the Hirer of its standard hiring policies and estimated associated charges.

4. General Conditions of Use of Center

4.1 TIMES OF EVENTS

The Hirer will commence and conclude the Hiring at the starting and finishing times and will ensure that, if applicable, the intervals take place all as specified in Item 6 of Schedule 1 unless such change shall have been previously approved in writing by the Licenser.

4.2 USE OF LICENSER'S STAFF

The Hirer will use only staff nominated or provided by the Licenser, and the Hirer will use subcontractors and further staff, whether employees of the Hirer or volunteer staff, only with the prior approval of the Licenser, which may in its absolute discretion disapprove any particular person.

4.3 INDUSTRIAL AWARDS

The Hirer will, in the use of any staff employed by the Licenser and in the employment or engagement of staff on its own account, observe and comply at all times with the provisions of all industrial agreements, awards, and determinations applicable from time to time in respect of any person or persons engaged or employed in the Center and/or in connection with the use of the License Area and will procure that all agents, subcontractors, consultants, and performers observe and comply at all times with the provisions of all such industrial agreements, awards, and determinations.

4.4 WORKPLACE HEALTH AND SAFETY ACT OF 1989

The Hirer will, in its use of the Center, in the use of any plant or equipment on or brought on to the Center, in the use of any staff employed by the Licenser, and in the employment or engagement of staff on its own account, and in all other respects comply at all times with the provisions of the Workplace Health and Safety Act of 1989 as amended from time to time and any regulations enacted pursuant to that act, and the Hirer will do so regardless of whether or not the said act or regulations places the direct responsibility therefore on the Licenser.

4.5 EMPLOYMENT POLICIES

The Hirer will comply with all employment policies laid down from time to time by the Licenser for the Center.

4.6 WORKERS' COMPENSATION

The Hirer warrants that the Hirer's staff employed by the Hirer at the Center and the staff of its servants, agents, and licensees employed at the Center and any volunteer workers associated with the Hiring will at all times while so employed or occupied be covered by applicable workers' compensation insurance, or the equivalent insurance for volunteer workers.

4.7 PROPER SUPERVISION

The Hirer will ensure that at all times its servants, agents, invitees, and licensees are properly supervised and are continuously under the direction and control of a person nominated by the Hirer for that purpose and approved by the Licenser, and such approval will not unreasonably be withheld.

4.8 MAKING EMPLOYEES AND OTHER PERSONS AWARE OF OBLIGATIONS

The Hirer agrees that it will make all of its servants, agents, subcontractors, invitees, licensees, players, performers, participants, exhibitors, and competitors who perform any work on its behalf at the Center or on the grounds of the Center or otherwise in relation to the Event aware of their respective obligations pursuant to the Workplace Health and Safety Act, and the Hirer agrees to procure that each of its servants, agents, invitees, licensees, players, performers, participants, exhibitors, and competitors will perform and observe all of such obligations as if they were parties hereto.

4.9 TECHNICAL QUESTIONNAIRE

The Hirer will, as soon as practicable following the signing of this Agreement, but before tickets are released for sale, and at least 30 days before the first date of the Event, deliver to the Licenser a fully completed technical questionnaire in the form attached in Schedule 7, setting out full particulars of the Hirer's technical, production, and labor requirements and will thereafter promptly inform the Licenser in writing of any proposed change or variation in those particulars. The Licenser shall retain the right to accept or approve such proposed change or variation or addition and may advise the Hirer of a change to the hiring charges or other charges or costs should the proposed changes be approved by the Licenser.

The Hirer warrants to the Licenser that the answers that it gives to the questions in the technical questionnaire shall be complete and accurate in all respects and shall fully disclose all of the Hirer's requirements in respect of the Hiring, and the Hirer acknowledges that the Licenser, in granting the License herein contained, is relying on the completeness and accuracy of such answers and such disclosures. In the event that any such answers are not complete and accurate in all respects or do not fully disclose the Hirer's requirements, the Hirer shall be deemed to have committed a breach of a fundamental obligation under this Agreement, entitling the Licenser, immediately on becoming aware that such answers are not complete and accurate in all respects or do not fully disclose the Hirer's requirements, to terminate this Agreement by notice to the Hirer without there being any further liability on the Licenser hereunder but without prejudice to all or any further or other rights that it may have against the Hirer, whether hereunder or otherwise.

4.10 GENERAL SECURITY AND KEYS

The Hirer will comply and will ensure that at all times its servants, agents, invitees, and licensees will comply with all requirements laid down by the Licenser from time to time in respect of the general security of the Center; will ensure that all keys to doors and equipment in the Center that are made available to the Hirer will be kept in charge of such persons as shall be authorized by the Licenser; will not make duplicate keys; and will deliver up all keys to the Licenser upon the Hirer's vacating the Center.

The Hirer will pay the cost of replacement of any key or lock lost or damaged by the Hirer, its servants, agents, invitees, or licensees during the term of the License and the cost of replacement of lock barrels for any lock where any key in the possession of the Hirer is lost and not returned at the end of the License Period.

4.11 DISORDERLY CONDUCT

The Hirer will conduct all events and other activities carried on by it in the License Area in a proper and orderly manner and will not permit or suffer any riotous, disorderly, or improper conduct in the Center or any part thereof nor permit or suffer any person who is guilty of riotous, disorderly, or improper conduct to be or remain on or in the Center nor permit or suffer to be done in or about the Center any act, matter, or thing which may injure or tend to injure the reputation of the Center or the Licenser.

4.12 CROWD CONTROL

The Hirer acknowledges and agrees that the Licenser will retain the sole rights to direct crowd control within the Center and shall be entitled to make all such arrangements and employ all such personnel as shall, in the opinion of the Licenser, be appropriate in order to ensure an efficient management of patrons of the Event in the Center. The Hirer acknowledges that it is the policy of the Licenser that at every Event conducted at the Center any Patron having been sold or otherwise provided with a ticket for a seat for an Event shall be entitled to a clear unobstructed view of the Event from that seat for the whole of the Event, and the Hirer agrees that it shall use its best endeavors to ensure that such policy is complied with in all respects during the Event and agrees, in particular, without limiting the generality of the foregoing, to ensure that persons participating in the Event do not behave in a disorderly manner or in a way that is offensive to any Patron or the Licenser and do not encourage Patrons to stand or move about the Center during the Event.

4.13 SECURITY SYSTEMS OR PROCEDURES

The Hirer acknowledges and agrees that the Licenser will have overall control of all security systems and security procedures as are necessary to ensure the security at all times of the Center and all persons in and facilities of the Center and shall be entitled to employ or engage from time to time such security personnel or special duty police as it deems fit to ensure such security.

4.14 HIRER TO COMPLY WITH SECURITY REQUIREMENTS

The Hirer will, and will ensure that its servants, agents, subcontractors, invitees, licensees, players, performers, participants, exhibitors, and competitors will, comply with all requirements of the Licenser from time to time in respect of the security of the Center and/or crowd control within the Center, and the Hirer hereby appoints the Licenser, its servants and agents, as agents of the Hirer, to refuse admission to or cause to be removed any person from the Center.

4.15 POLICE LIAISON

The Hirer acknowledges and agrees that it will be the responsibility of the Licenser to conduct liaison with police in respect of the attendance by members of the police force at the Center or any part thereof as and when required, and the Hirer will not hinder or obstruct or permit or suffer to be hindered or obstructed any member of the police force or any security officer or attendant or other employee or agent of the Licenser in his/her activities within the Center from time to time.

4.16 EMERGENCY SERVICES

The Hirer will not, and will ensure that its servants, agents, invitees, and licensees will not, hinder or obstruct any member of the medical or nursing profession, police force, any fire brigade, ambulance service, first aid service or other emergency service, or any security officer employed in respect of the Center in the exercise of his/her duties in or about the Center. If the Hirer or its servants, agents, subcontractors, invitees, licensees, players, performers, participants, exhibitors, and competitors or any Patron in or about the Center shall at any time accept or use the services of a physician or surgeon, or accept or use any ambulance service or any service in connection with any injury or sickness occurring to any person or persons while within or about the Center during the term of this Agreement even though such service or services be made available or be obtained through the Licenser, the Hirer accepts full responsibility for the acts and conduct, or services rendered, of any physician or surgeon or ambulance service or other service and will hold the Licenser harmless from all responsibility or liability thereof.

4.17 OBSERVANCE OF SECURITY AND EVACUATION PROCEDURES

The Hirer will ensure that its servants, agents, subcontractors, invitees, licensees, players, performers, participants, exhibitors, and competitors will make themselves familiar with all emergency evacuation procedures of the Center and will observe all security and emergency evacuation procedures applicable from time to time in respect of the Center or any part thereof.

4.18 CONCESSIONS

The Hirer acknowledges and agrees that the Licenser shall have the sole right to sell or distribute in the Center wines, spirits, and other beverages (whether alcoholic or not), refreshments, food, confectionery, tobacco, cigars, cigarettes, or other articles or services and that the Licenser may adopt such means as it deems fit for the sale or distribution thereof (including but not limited to the appointment of such agents or distributors as the Licenser may deem fit). All revenue derived from the sale of such items shall be retained by the Licenser. The Hirer agrees that it will not and will procure that its servants, agents, subcontractors, invitees, licensees, players, perform-ers, participants, exhibitors, and competitors will not bring into, receive, or provide any such items in the Center.

4.19 MERCHANDISING

The Hirer acknowledges and agrees that the Licenser shall have the sole right to sell or distribute in the Center any other merchandising items not covered by Clause 4.18, and the Licenser may adopt such means as it deems fit for the sale or distribution thereof (including but not limited to the appointment of such agents or distributors as the Licenser may deem fit). Notwithstanding the foregoing, the Licenser may in its absolute discretion appoint the Hirer as its agent for the sale or distribution of such items, and the Hirer may subject to its obtaining the prior approval of the Licenser nominate a subagent to undertake merchandising of items on its behalf. The Licenser shall be entitled to pay money directly to such subagent unless the Hirer shall have required the Licenser by notice in writing to pay such moneys being proceeds from the sale of such merchandising items directly to the Hirer.

If the Hirer falls to nominate a subagent and advise the Licenser of such subagent at least seven (7) days prior to the commencement of the License Period, the Licenser shall be entitled to deal directly with such person as it considers proper to deal with, where either:

4.19.1. The Licenser is reasonably of the opinion that such person has some form of approval from the Hirer, in which case the Licenser will be entitled to assume that such person is the subagent of the Hirer; or

4.19.2. The Licenser is reasonably of the opinion that such person pro-poses to supply merchandise in connection with the Event.

The Licenser may, at any time, advise the Hirer that the Licenser is not prepared to deal directly with the Hirer's subagent in relation to the sale of merchandising items, and the Licenser shall be entitled to deal directly with the Hirer.

4.20 SAFE AND PROPER USE OF LICENSE AREA

The Hirer will, and will ensure that its servants, agents, invitees, and licens-ees will, use the License Area and its facilities and its equipment in a safe, proper, and efficient manner so as not to involve any appreciable risk of injury to persons or damage to property in or near the Center to the satisfac-tion of the Licenser and will immediately comply with any reasonable direc-tion of the Licenser in connection with the safe and proper use of the License Area, its facilities, and equipment. Nothing in this Agreement will transfer any responsibility for the safe conduct of the Event or the safe and proper use of the License Area, its facilities, and equipment from the Hirer to the Licenser, nor will it require the Licenser to give any directions whatsoever in relation to the safe and proper use of the License Area, its facilities, and equipment. No reasonable directions given by the Licenser in good faith will release the Hirer from any further obligations under this Agreement.

4.21 TECHNICAL AND SAFETY APPROVAL

The Hirer will not install or bring into the License Area any additional electrical installation equipment or fittings or any flammable, explosive, or other dangerous goods unless the same and the use and storage thereof comply in all respects with all relevant statutes, regulations, bylaws, and ordinances and unless such installation, equipment, fittings, or goods have been previously approved by the Licenser and have passed such additional, technical, and/or safety inspections as the Licenser may in its absolute discretion require. Nothing in this Agreement will require the Licenser to undertake such inspections. The fact that the Licenser does undertake any such inspection will not release the Hirer from any of its obligations under this Agreement, nor will it release it from any duty of care which it may owe to the Licenser or to any other person whatsoever. The Licenser shall be entitled to retain technical advisers and experts to advise it on the staging of any Event, and the fees of such advisers and experts shall be at the cost of the Hirer.

4.22 FIRE-PROOFING OF ITEMS

The Hirer will not bring into the Center any scenery, curtains, equipment, or other property unless the same have been fire-proofed (where required) in accordance with the prevailing fire code in the state of _____ and/or prescribed by the Licenser from time to time, and any safety standard presented by or requirement of the Licenser and the Hirer will thereafter maintain such items in a fire-proofed condition to the satisfaction of the Licenser while the same remain in the Center.

4.23 SAFETY STANDARDS IN EQUIPMENT

The Hirer will not bring into the Center or use in the Center any equipment or materials of any kind whatsoever unless the state of same is in accordance with any prevailing safety standard or requirement in the state of _____, and the Hirer will thereafter maintain such items in a condition that complies with any relevant safety standard or requirement to the satisfaction of the Licenser while the same remain at the Center. The Hirer further agrees to apply for, obtain, and for the whole of the Hiring maintain all registrations, licenses, approvals, or consents that are required in respect of the use or operation of any such equipment or materials pursuant to any statute, regulations, bylaws, or ordinances.

4.24 SAFETY STANDARDS IN STAGING

The Hirer will, in staging the Hiring, comply with all the safety standards and requirements (if any) imposed by the Licenser or any statutory or other relevant authority from time to time and will apply for, obtain, and for the whole of the Hiring maintain all registrations, licenses, approvals, and consents that are required by statute, regulations, bylaws, or ordinances in order to enable it to comply with its obligations under this Subclause.

4.25 EQUIPMENT INGRESS AND EGRESS

The Hirer will ensure that articles, fittings, fixtures, materials, and equipment shall be brought into or removed from the Center only at entrances and exits designated by the Licenser. The Licenser shall have the right to determine the total number and weight of vehicles that may enter the Center at any one time, the total weight of all items that may be brought into the Center or any part of the Center, and the total number and weight of the items that may be lifted on individual hoists at any one time, and the Licenser shall also have the sole right to determine what area if any may be used for such vehicles and/or items.

4.26 EQUIPMENT, DECORATIONS, AND FURNISHINGS

The Hirer will not install any equipment or temporary decorations or furnishings in the License Area or suspend or permit to be suspended any object or thing from the ceiling or from any wall of the License Area without the prior approval in writing of the Licenser, such approval not being unreasonably withheld, and any rigging, electrical connections, or other work will be performed only by or under the supervision of the Licenser, its staff, or agent. The fact that the Licenser or its staff or agent supervises such work will not release the Hirer from any of its obligations under this Agreement nor will it release the Hirer from any duty of care that it may owe to the Licenser or to any other person whatsoever.

4.27 ALTERATIONS AND ADDITIONS

The Hirer will not make any alteration or addition to the structure or the fittings, facilities, or equipment of the Center without the prior written consent of the Licenser, and such approval will not unreasonably be withheld.

4.28 CHANGEOVER

The normal mode of use of the Center is the full concert mode, which incorporates seating for approximately 10,000 persons, including fixed seating and temporary stalls seating. To the extent not otherwise provided herein, the Hirer agrees to reimburse the Licenser for all costs of labor and materials incurred in changing the Center from the normal mode to the Hirer's required mode for the Event and in changing the Center after the Event to the normal mode.

4.29 DESIGN OF WORKS AND STRUCTURES

The Hirer warrants to the Licenser that all due care has been exercised in the design of any works or structures to be constructed in the Center or the grounds of the Center and that all due care will be exercised during such construction, and the Hirer agrees to indemnify and to keep the Licenser indemnified against any loss, damage, claim, demand, penalty, fine, or charge that is suffered by or imposed upon the Licenser directly or indirectly in consequence of any defect of design, defect in construction, defective materials, or faulty workmanship in such construction.

4.30 HIRER TO VACATE

The Hirer will, directly after the completion of the last Event of the Hiring, and in any event prior to the "time by which the Hirer must be clear of the Center" at end of License Period specified in Item 5 of Schedule 1, remove from the Center the following:

i.   All additional equipment, decorations, or furnishings installed pursuant to Clause 4.25;
ii. All additional electrical installation, equipment, or fittings installed pursuant to Clause 4.20;
iii. All sets, costumes, properties, equipment, and all other goods of any kind whatsoever that have been brought into the Center by the Hirer, its servants, agents, invitees, or licensees.

4.31 UPON VACATION

Upon vacating the Center the Hirer will do the following:

i.   Leave the Center and its facilities and equipment in a clean, safe, and proper condition to the reasonable satisfaction of the Licenser;
ii. Restore at its own cost all sound, lighting, and staging apparatus to the basic standard arrangement as prescribed by the Licenser from time to time to the reasonable satisfaction of the Licenser;
iii. If required by the Licenser, remove any alterations or additions made to the structure, fittings, facilities, or equipment of the Center pursuant to Clause 4.26 and, at its own cost, restore such structure, fittings, facilities, or equipment to its original state prior to such alteration or additions being made; and
iv. Comply with its obligations pursuant to Clause 7.

4.32 FAILURE TO REMOVE GOODS, EQUIPMENT, AND OTHER ITEMS

In the event that the Hirer fails to comply with all or any of its obligations pursuant to Clauses 4.29 and 4.30, the Licenser may, in its discretion at the sole risk and expense of the Hirer, remove any or all such items from the License Area and store same. The Hirer will pay to the Licenser the storage charges thereby incurred by the Licenser, or if the items are stored by the Licenser itself, the normal prevailing market charges payable in respect of such storage as well as charges for movement of goods elsewhere and associated costs of movement and/or storage, including insurance and the Licenser's staff costs.

The remedies provided by this Subclause and Subclause 3.6 may both apply and are not mutually exclusive, save that the Hirer shall not be obliged to pay additional rental pursuant to Subclause 3.6 by reason only of not having removed certain equipment from the License Area to the extent to which such equipment has been dealt with pursuant to this Subclause.

4.33 HIRER'S PUBLIC RISK INSURANCE

The Hirer and its agents, nominees, and licensees will carry their own public risk insurance with an insurer or insurers approved by the Licenser and in such form as is approved by the Licenser for a minimum amount of $5,000,000 (five million dollars), or such other amount as is specified in Schedule 4 amended to this Agreement or such other amount as the Licenser may from time to time during the Hiring reasonably require and will provide a copy of the policy and a certificate of currency of insurance seven (7) days prior to the Event and nominate the Licenser on any such policy as an additional insured. Where the Hirer is unable to present such policy and such endorsed certificate of currency of insurance or such policy is not in a form acceptable to the Licenser, the Hirer hereby appoints the Licenser, if the Licenser so desires, to automatically apply to such insurer as the Licenser shall in its discretion determine for public risk insurance coverage on the Hirer's behalf in such amount as the Licenser shall in its discretion determine, and the Hirer shall be liable for all premiums, charges, duties, and other amounts payable in respect of such insurance and shall immediately on demand being made by the Licenser pay to the Licenser any such amounts that the Licenser pays on the Hirer's behalf. Nothing in this Clause will require the Licenser to apply for such insurance on the Hirer's behalf, nor will it require any insurer to accept any such application, nor will it release the Hirer from its absolute responsibility under this Agreement to arrange on his/her own behalf the required public risk insurance.

4.34 FURTHER INSURANCE REQUIREMENTS

The Hirer will not, and will ensure that its servants, agents, invitees, and licensees will not, without the written authority of the Licenser, do or suffer to be done anything in the Center whereby any policy of insurance on the Center, its facilities, or equipment or in respect of the use or occupation of the

Center or any part thereof by any person may be or become void or voidable or whereby the rate of premium thereon may be increased. The Hirer will pay to the Licenser on demand all amounts payable by way of costs or increased insurance premiums on any policy of insurance so affected. The Hirer, prior to the License Period, will produce to the Licenser a certificate of currency of any cancellation of events or nonperformance insurance held by the Hirer or such other contract insuring the fulfillment of the provisions of this Agreement, and in the instance of nonappearance, postponement, or cancellation of the Event, the Hirer will forthwith provide the Licenser with a copy of such insurance policy.

4.35 INSURANCE AGAINST ALL RISKS

The Hirer hereby covenants that it will at all times maintain sufficient insurance with an insurer or insurers approved by the Licenser to indemnify it against any loss or damage that it may suffer or to which it may be exposed whether by reason of the Hiring, the conduct of any Event, or the terms hereof.

4.36 POSTERS, SIGNS, AND ADVERTISING MATERIAL

The Hirer will not, without the prior written consent of the Licenser, display any posters, signs, or advertising materials in the following places:

i.   Any part of the Center; or
ii. Any other place that may bring action against or disrepute to the Licenser or the Center or be in breach of any relevant regulations.

Further, the Licenser reserves the right to display its own signage within the arena, and the location and presentation of such signage shall be at the discretion of the Licenser.

4.37 PUBLICITY AND ADVERTISING INFORMATION

In all advertising, publicity, and promotion for the Event, the Hirer, its employees, servants, agents, and representatives will ensure that the details provided in Schedule 6 will be used, when applicable.

The Hirer, when requested by the Licenser, will submit all advertising and promotional material to the Licenser for approval prior to publication and will ensure that the format of ticket booking and Center details meets the Licenser's standard requirements and reviewed requirements from time to time.

The Hirer will indemnify the Licenser, its employees, servants, agents, representatives, and subcontractors against any claims whatsoever from any person or regulatory authority regarding the publication of any material relating to the Event.

4.38 PERFORMING RIGHTS AND COPYRIGHT INDEMNITY

The Hirer hereby agrees to indemnify and keep indemnified the Licenser from and against all actions, claims, demands, losses, damages, costs, and expenses arising from or incurred directly or indirectly by reason of any infringement or alleged infringement of copyright or other protected right, or any act, default, or omission by the Hirer, or the Hirer's servants, agents, licensees, or other persons connected with the Hirer or the Event.

4.39 PHOTOGRAPHS, SOUND, TELEVISION RECORDING, VIDEO DISPLAY

4.39.1. The Hirer will not, except with the prior approval of the Licenser, and then only in such circumstances and subject to such conditions as shall have been approved by the Licenser, take or permit or suffer to be taken any photograph or film, video, sound, or television recording or transmission (whether or not for commercial purposes) in the Center and shall not transmit or reproduce or permit or allow the transmission or reproduction by television broadcast, video, or sound broadcast or by any other means of any Event that takes place within the Center unless the prior approval of the Licenser has been obtained and a written agreement relating to the same has been entered into between the Licenser and the Hirer. Such separate agreement may contain but shall not be limited to provisions governing the right of the Licenser to be paid a fee and/or a royalty in respect thereof and the places in which any equipment can be positioned.

4.39.2. If the Licenser so requires, the Hirer will approve the operation of the Center's in-house video monitor system to display the Event on the various monitors placed throughout the Center for the convenience of Patrons. The Licenser warrants to the Hirer that except with the Hirer's express permission or direction the Licenser will not in any way record or transmit any Event other than for display on the in-house video system.

4.40 ACCESS OF PERSONNEL

The Licenser, its officers, directors, servants, employees, and agents shall at all times have free access to all parts of the Center. Subject to the Licenser's approval as to numbers, the Hirer may issue media passes, car passes, and backstage passes permitting specified persons access to specified areas of the Center normally closed to the public. No person so authorized by the Hirer, other than persons actively engaged in the presentation of the Event, shall enter the auditorium without having been issued with a ticket for a seat in the auditorium.

4.41 ANNOUNCEMENTS DURING PERFORMANCES

The Licenser, at such reasonable time or times as it may deem appropriate, may announce, describe, and advertise over any sound system and closed circuit television system in the Center during the staging of the Event, including, without limitation, announcements, descriptions, and advertisements concerning other or future events being or to be held in the Center or elsewhere, and the Licenser reserves and retains the exclusive right to use and may use the Center's sound system, closed circuit television system, display advertising capabilities and facilities and all other advertising capabilities and facilities in and about the Center in any places which in its opinion, which shall be conclusive, are desirable or appropriate, providing only that such announcements, descriptions, advertisements, and use do not, in the opinion of the Licenser, unduly disrupt or interfere with the staging of the Event.

4.42 DETERMINATION OF SOUND LEVELS

The Licenser shall have sole authority to determine the sound level limit that is acceptable within the Center but shall be under no obligation to the Hirer to determine such levels.

4.43 COMPLIANCE WITH RULES, REGULATIONS OF THE CENTER

The Hirer will and shall ensure that its servants, agents, subcontractors, invitees, licensees, players, performers, participants, exhibitors, and competitors shall at all times comply with the terms of this Agreement, and also comply with all reasonable requests, directions, rules, regulations, ordinances, notices, announcements, or requirements made, given, published, or enacted by the Licenser and/or the Council from time to time in respect of the Center and the use thereof or any part thereof, and the Hirer, its servants, agents, subcontractors, invitees, licensees, players, performers, participants, exhibitors, and competitors will use every effort to direct and ensure the compliance of all Patrons therewith and will not invite or knowingly allow any person, including a Patron, to breach or contravene such terms, requests, directions, rules, regulations, ordinances, notices, announcements, or requirements.

4.44 JEOPARDIZING OF LICENSES

The Hirer will not do or suffer to be done anything whereby any license or permit issued or in force in respect of the lawful management or operation of the Center or any part thereof may be or become liable to be forfeited or suspended or the renewal thereof refused.

4.45 OBSERVANCE OF LEGISLATION AND GOVERNMENT PERMITS

The Hirer shall obtain at its expense all government, semigovernment, and local authority permits, licenses, consents, and approvals that are required for the use or operation of any equipment, machinery, structure, and any other thing whatsoever used in connection with the Event or for the construction of any works or structures in the Center or the grounds surrounding the Center and agrees in all respects to observe and perform all conditions attaching to such permits, licenses, consents, and approvals. The Hirer further agrees to perform and observe all obligations that are placed on a person using or operating any such equipment, machinery, structure, or thing or on a person constructing any such works or structure or on a person presenting the Event by any government, semigovernment, or local authority legislation, regulation, ordinance, or bylaw and regardless of whether such legislation, regulation, ordinance, or bylaw places the direct responsibility therefore on the Council, the Licenser, the Hirer, or on any other person the Hirer agrees to indemnify the Licenser against any loss, damage (including consequential loss or damage), claim, penalty, fine, or charge suffered by or imposed on the Licenser directly or indirectly in consequence of the Hirer's failing so to do.

4.46 REHEARSALS

If the Hirer desires to use the Center for rehearsals, setting up of the Center for the staging of the Event, or for a performance prior to the delivery of possession by the Licenser, it shall notify the Licenser in writing. The Licenser and the Hirer may agree in writing on such additional dates, and unless expressly stated to the contrary, the terms of such hiring shall be on the terms of this Agreement. The charges for such hiring shall be specified by the Licenser, and the Hirer will reimburse the Licenser for any additional costs or expenses incurred as a result of such hiring.

4.47 FURTHER OBLIGATIONS OF HIRER

The Hirer shall do the following:

i.   Supply and pay for all, servants, agents, subcontractors, players, performers, participants, exhibitors, and competitors required for the proper presentation of the Event;
ii. Transport all personnel, properties, facilities, and equipment necessary for the Event to and from the Center;
iii. Present the Event in the most advantageous manner and style practicable; and
iv. Pay all government charges, taxes, and levies due as a result of the Event by the due dates for payment thereof.

4.48 NONEXCLUSIVE USE

The Hirer acknowledges that in addition to the use of the Center provided for in this Agreement, the Center and various parts thereof and areas therein may be used for the installation, holding or presentation, and removal of activities, events, and engagements other than the Event and that in order for the Center to operate as efficiently as practicable it may be necessary for the use or availability of services and facilities of the Center, including, without limitation, entrances, exits, truck ramps, receiving areas, marshaling areas, storage areas, passenger or freight elevators, and concession areas, to be scheduled or shared. The Hirer agrees that the Licenser shall have full, complete, and absolute authority to establish the schedules for the use and availability of such services and facilities and to determine when and the extent to which the sharing of such services and facilities is necessary or desirable, and the Hirer agrees to comply with any schedules so established and to cooperate in any sharing arrangements so determined. In no circumstances shall the Hirer enter or use any areas, services, facilities, or parts of the Center other than those parts of the Center made available under the terms of this Agreement without first obtaining the Licenser's consent and approval.

4.49 POLITICAL PURPOSES

The Hirer shall not use the Center for any political purpose whatsoever unless the Event itself has been expressly advised by the Hirer to the Licenser to be political. If this provision shall be breached, the Licenser shall be entitled to withhold from moneys otherwise payable by the Licenser to the Hirer such reasonable amount as will compensate the Licenser for injury to its property, including any loss of goodwill.

4.50 COLLECTIONS

No collections, whether for charity or otherwise, shall be made or attempted to be made prior to, during, or after any performance staged by the Hirer at the Center without the written permission of the Licenser.

5. Tickets

5.1 TICKETS TO BE SOLD BY LICENSER

The Hirer acknowledges and agrees that in order for the Licenser:

i.   To meet the security and audit requirements placed on it by the Management Agreement;
ii. To maintain the highest operational standards; and
iii. To estimate the License Charge specified in Schedule 2, all tickets in respect of any Event will be sold or otherwise made available by the Licenser as agent for the Hirer and that the Licenser may adopt such means as it thinks fit for the sale of tickets (including but not limited to the appointment of such subagents as the Licenser may think fit for the sale of tickets).

The Hirer agrees that as between the Licenser and the Hirer, the Hirer shall be bound to perform all obligations owed to the purchasers of tickets sold or otherwise made available by the Licenser as if the same had been sold by the Hirer and the Hirer had received valuable consideration in respect of the sale thereof, and the Hirer agrees to indemnify the Licenser and keep the Licenser indemnified in respect of all loss, damage, and consequential loss and damage, including but not limited to loss of profit arising directly or indirectly out of the Licenser's selling or otherwise making available tickets as agent for the Hirer.

5.2 CONDITIONS OF SALE OF TICKETS

Unless otherwise specified in Schedule 4 amended to this Agreement, the Hirer acknowledges that the standard conditions of sale and terms of admittance, detailed as follows, will appear on the reverse of tickets for the Event.

NOTICE AND AGREEMENT CONDITIONS OF SALE AND TERMS OF ADMITTANCE

This ticket is a personal revocable license and is sold by _____ and _____ or its outlets solely as agent for and on behalf of the organization, venue management, or promoter ("the Seller") responsible for the event, performance, game, or service ("the Event") for which it is valid. Any complaints regarding the Event will be directed to the Seller. This ticket cannot be exchanged, refunded, or returned after purchase or replaced if lost, stolen, damaged, or destroyed, except as the Entertainment Industry Code of Fair Practices expressly prohibits the resale of this ticket at any price in excess of the initial purchase price. Any prohibited sale will render the ticket invalid, and legal action will follow.

This ticket is sold subject to the Seller's Conditions of Sale and Terms of Admittance, a copy of which is available for inspection at the time of purchase of this ticket, and notice of such items and conditions will be displayed at the entrance to the venue on the day of the Event. To the extent that they are not inconsistent with the Seller's conditions and terms, the holder of this ticket ("the Holder") is admitted on the following conditions.

By use of this ticket the Holder agrees and warrants that if under the legal drinking age, he/she will not attempt to purchase and/or consume any alcohol at the venue of the Event and if of age he/she will not consume such quantity of alcohol as shall give rise to a blood reading above his/her ability to drive a motor vehicle, whichever is the lesser. Club patrons agree to abide by all club bylaws.

The Holder agrees to being subject to a search for any prohibited items, including but not limited to weapons; controlled, dangerous, and illegal substances; alcohol; bottles, cans, or coolers; recording equipment; still, video, or movie cameras, which may be expressly forbidden and subject to confiscation.

The Holder will not transmit or aid in transmitting any description, picture, account, or reproduction of the Event. The Holder grants permission to the Seller and its agents to utilize the Holder's image or likeness incidental to any photographic record, live or recorded video display, or any other transmission or reproduction in whole or in part of the Event.

The Holder voluntarily assumes all risk and danger incidental to the Event whether occurring prior to, during, or subsequent to the actual Event, including damage or injury caused by other Holders.

The Holder of a ticket purchased at a concessional price must be prepared to produce proof of age or documentation justifying the concession when the ticket is presented for use. Latecomers may not be admitted until a suitable break in the Event.

The Seller reserves the right to refuse admission without explanation and to eject any person whose conduct the Seller or its agent deems disorderly or offensive without compensation. The Seller reserves the right, in good faith, to add, withdraw, or substitute artists or competitors, change seating arrangements and audience capacity, and to announce a change of venue and/or vary advertised programs as necessary. Seller may cancel, interrupt, or stop the Event because of adverse weather, dangerous situations, or any other causes beyond its reasonable control, and such cancellation, interruption, or stopping of the Event shall not entitle the Holder to make any claim whatsoever except for a ticket for a replacement Event if scheduled, or a refund of ticket price if Event is canceled and not subsequently rescheduled.

5.3 SALE OF TICKETS

The printing, distribution, and sale of all tickets in respect of any Hiring will be under the general supervision of the Licenser and will be carried out by the Licenser or by the person or persons nominated by the Licenser. The Licenser, its servants, agents, and subcontractors shall not be liable to the Hirer for any loss arising from any failure in any ticketing system or any other matter affecting the sale of tickets beyond the reasonable control of the Licenser. The Hirer shall not be entitled to sell or otherwise make available any tickets for the Event without first obtaining the written consent of the Licenser, which may, at the absolute discretion of the Licenser, be granted, withheld, or granted subject to such conditions as the Licenser shall determine, including, without leaving the generality of the foregoing, a condition that the Hirer deliver to the Licenser a written statement with each payment made to the Licenser pursuant to Clause 5.4 (or if no payment is due pursuant to Clause 5.4 then daily) signed on behalf of the Hirer setting out the details of the number of tickets sold by the Hirer and the price at which such tickets are sold.

The Hirer shall not be entitled to appoint or approve any person or persons to conduct the sale or resale of any tickets for an Event, other than those nominated or specifically approved in writing by the Licenser.

The Licenser shall determine in its absolute discretion the manner of payment for the purchase of tickets for the Hirer's Event (including whether a particular credit/debit card or credit/debit card facility is an acceptable method of payment).

The Hirer specifically agrees that no person or persons other than those approved by the Licenser will be permitted to sell or resell any ticket for the Event at any price exceeding the purchase price of a ticket as originally exhibited on the face of the ticket.

The Hirer specifically authorizes the Licenser to, in its absolute discretion, recall or render invalid any tickets sold, resold, or resupplied in contravention of the above requirement and to refuse access to the holder of such a ticket to the Event. The Hirer further agrees to indemnify the Licenser from any claim or costs incurred by the Licenser in the fulfillment of this authorization.

5.4 DEEMED SALE OF TICKETS

If a ticket is drawn by the Hirer or its employees, servants, agents, or representatives and then transacted by the Hirer in any way for cash or contra (tickets in exchange for services provided), such transaction shall be deemed a sale of the ticket at the full adult ticket price, and the Licenser shall receive the amount due to it as part of the License Charge. If tickets drawn by the Hirer, its employees, servants, agents, or representatives are sold for cash, gross receipts therefore are to be paid by the Hirer to the Licenser within twenty-four (24) hours of their receipt by the Hirer or within such other period as is approved by the Licenser. Any sale for cash shall be made at standard ticket prices notified by the Hirer to the Licenser pursuant to Clause 5.7 unless otherwise approved by the Licenser.

5.5 TICKET SALES OUTLETS

All sales of tickets shall be made at the Box Office or offices maintained by the Licenser and at such other sales outlets as shall be provided by the Licenser or by any person nominated by the Licenser to carry out the sale of such tickets.

5.6 FORM OF TICKETS

The tickets will be printed on such paper stock, and include terms, exclusions, and conditions on the face or reverse side as required by the Licenser for security, audit, and operational reasons.

5.7 SUPPLY OF TICKET INFORMATION

The Hirer will deliver to the Licenser as soon as practicable after the signing of this Agreement full particulars of the following:

i.   The information that the Hirer requests should appear on the face of the tickets;
ii. The gross sale prices (inclusive of such system booking fee as is specified by the Licenser to the Hirer) for which the tickets are to be sold and the price barriers (if any, as approved by the Licenser) in respect of which same are to be sold; and
iii. The persons or classes of persons who are to receive complimentary tickets or tickets at concessional prices, and the Licenser will make available

such information to the person nominated as provided in Clause 5.3 to arrange for printing and distribution of all such tickets who will thereafter cause such tickets to be available for sale under the normal commercial arrangements of the Licenser and of the person nominated as provided in Clause 5.3.

5.8 RETENTION OF TICKETS FOR COUNCIL
Tickets will be made available to the Council for its exclusive use and without any cost on the part of the Council for that area and/or that number of seats (if any) designated in Item 1 of Schedule 3 in respect of the agreed use of the Center by the Hirer.

5.9 RETENTION OF TICKETS FOR LICENSER (FOR APPROVED SALE)
Tickets will be withheld from sale and distribution in respect of that area and/or those seats which are specified in Item 2 of Schedule 3 on the basis of the following:

i.   If any of the approved sale tickets remain unsold seven (7) days prior to the date of each performance, then one half of those tickets remaining will be released for general sale; and
ii. The remaining tickets for each performance may be released for general sale by the Licenser after twelve (12) noon on the day of each Event.

Up until those times the Licenser or his nominee may purchase all or any of the said tickets at usual prices *provided always that* the Licenser will not incur any liability to the Hirer whatsoever in respect of such tickets after they have been made available for sale or distribution in accordance with this Agreement.

5.10 RETENTION OF TICKETS FOR LICENSER (HOUSE SEATS)
Tickets will be withheld from sale and distribution in respect of that area and/or those seats which are specified in Item 3 of Schedule 3 for the exclusive use of the Licenser, and any tickets unallocated by the Licenser may be released for sale after twelve (12) noon on the day of each Event.

5.11 RETENTION OF TICKETS FOR HIRER
The Hirer may allocate up to four percent (4%) of the total tickets available for each Event as complimentary tickets. Any additional allocation of complimentary tickets by the Hirer will be made only with the consent of the Licenser; otherwise any such tickets so allocated or any tickets from the

complimentary allocation subsequently offered for sale or exchanged for contra will be presumed to be sold at the full adult price by the Hirer for purposes of calculation of License charges and additional rentals pursuant to Clause 3. The total seats retained for the Hirer will be that area and/or those seats designated in Item 4 of Schedule 3, or as requested by the Hirer, and agreed in writing by the Licenser from time to time.

The Hirer shall not supply or sell or be knowingly concerned in the supply or sale of any tickets (whether tickets forming part of the allocation of complimentary tickets to the Hirer or tickets otherwise acquired by the Hirer) to any individual or organization for resupply or resale without the consent, in writing, of the Licenser.

The Hirer specifically authorizes the Licenser to, in its absolute discretion, recall or render invalid any tickets resold or resupplied for any deemed consideration from the Hirer's complimentary allocation by any person or persons without the consent, in writing, of the Licenser. The Hirer further agrees to indemnify the Licenser from any claim or costs incurred by the Licenser in the fulfillment of this authorization.

5.12 BOOKINGS HOLDINGS

Gross Box Office Proceeds for the Event must be deposited in the Licenser's nominated Bookings Holding Account in a secure financial institution selected by the Licenser, and the Licenser will be entitled in its absolute discretion at any time thereafter to apply the moneys as follows:

i.   If necessary, in refunds to holders of tickets; and/or
ii. In whole or partial discharge of any liability of the Hirer to the Licenser under this Agreement and/or of any liability of the Hirer arising in connection with or incidental to the Hiring, or otherwise.

It is fundamental to the estimation of the License Charge specified in Schedule 2 that any interest income earned in the Bookings Holding Account of the Licenser may at the absolute discretion of the Licenser either be retained in whole or in part by the Licenser for its sole benefit or applied in whole or in part in such manner as the Licenser shall in its discretion determine unless specifically detailed otherwise in the Variation to Standard Form Agreement in Schedule 4.

5.13 NO RESPONSIBILITY FOR PURCHASE FRAUD

Nothing in this Agreement will be interpreted as making the Licenser or any of its servants, agents, or licensees liable to the Hirer for any losses in revenue in respect of tickets due to fraud or nonpayment by the purchaser, and any payments voided or refunded to a purchaser will be claimed against the Hirer.

5.14 BOOKING FEE REIMBURSEMENT UPON CANCELLATION

If for any reason whatsoever the Event is canceled, the Hirer will immediately arrange an announcement to the public and schedule advertising advising of such cancellation to a level approved by the Licenser. Unless otherwise advised, full ticket refunds (including agency fees and telephone booking or subscription service fees) will be available to ticket-holders from the point of sale only, and the Hirer will pay to the Licenser upon demand an amount equal to the total booking fees income from the sale of tickets for the Event at the date of cancellation plus an additional amount equal to the abovementioned booking fees to facilitate refunds of tickets plus reimbursement of any costs incurred by the Licenser in facilitating the refunds of tickets or the advertising of such cancellation.

5.15 GROSS BOX OFFICE PROCEEDS

All Gross Box Office Receipts will be and shall remain the absolute property of the Licenser. Gross Box Office Proceeds shall first be applied by the Licenser in satisfaction of any remaining obligation or liability of the Hirer to the Licenser under this Agreement or otherwise.

The aforesaid applications shall be deemed to have been made as and when the said amounts become due, irrespective of the date upon which such applications shall be made upon the books of the Licenser. When the License Charge is based on a percentage of ticket sales, the portion attributable to each ticket sale shall be deemed due to the Licenser as each ticket is sold or transacted.

5.16 SETTLEMENT WITH THE HIRER

Within twenty-four (24) hours after the conclusion of the final performance of the Event the Licenser shall furnish the Hirer with a Box Office statement and at the Hirer's request make a provisional settlement with the Hirer with the Licenser withholding such reasonable amounts from such provisional settlement as it deems required to assure proper final settlement. Within seven (7) days after the final performance of the Event the Licenser shall furnish to the Hirer a statement showing all Gross Box Office Proceeds relating to the Hirer's use of the Center hereunder and the application of same, and the Licenser shall pay to the Hirer such moneys as shall be due to the Hirer. The Hirer agrees to examine such statement and to notify the Licenser in writing of any error in the statement or of any objection to any charge within five (5) business days after delivery of such statement, and unless the Hirer shall so notify the Licenser of such claimed error or objection within five (5) business days, such statement shall be deemed to be a true and correct statement of the account between the Licenser and the Hirer, and finalization of the account between the Hirer and the Licenser shall thereupon be deemed to have occurred. The Hirer agrees to pay promptly any amounts shown to be due to the Licenser on such statement that are not paid by the application of Gross Box Office Proceeds.

5.17 HIRER TO ADVISE SIGHTLINES

Before tickets for the Event are released for distribution or sale, the Hirer will clearly mark on the box plan attached in Schedule 5 the stage location or performance area, the stage plan including equipment placements and measurements, and the proposed sound mixing and lighting control positions and the dimensions and height thereof.

The Hirer will also clearly indicate the proposed position and dimensions of any other items involved with the Event that may in any way affect sightlines for Patrons of the Event.

The Hirer will then clearly mark the seats that the Hirer requests be distributed or sold to the public, which such seats having full, clear sightlines of the entire Event.

The Hirer will present the marked-up box plan and stage lay-out to the Licenser before tickets for the Event are released for sale or distribution, and the Hirer warrants to the Licenser that he has satisfied himself that all seating areas marked for sale or distribution will have full, clear sightlines of the Event, and the Hirer undertakes to ensure the full and clear sightlines of the Event for all seats so marked. The Licenser may withhold from sale certain seating areas marked for sale or distribution by the Hirer and may request from the Hirer further information or details displaying or guaranteeing the adequacy of sightlines for the Event, and the Hirer agrees to provide such details promptly to facilitate ticket sales or distribution of seats of the Event.

5.18 REFUND OF PURCHASE PRICE

The Licenser may at its discretion refund to any or all of the purchasers of tickets to the Event moneys paid in respect of the purchase of such ticket or tickets or part of such moneys, and the Licenser shall be under no liability to the Hirer under this Agreement or otherwise in respect of the moneys so refunded. Such refund may include all moneys paid by such purchasers in connection with the purchase of a ticket, including such moneys as shall be recoverable by the Licenser from the Hirer. The Licenser shall be entitled to offer a purchaser a replacement ticket to the Center for any performance of the Event or a performance of any other Event to be staged at the Center to the satisfaction of the purchaser in lieu of a refund.

5.19 INDEMNITY BY HIRER
If the Event is canceled due to any breach by the Hirer of the terms of this Agreement or any other default by the Hirer, the Hirer shall indemnify the Licenser, its employees, servants, agents, and subcontractors in respect of any claim that may be brought against the Licenser by any person or company who has purchased tickets for the Event.

5.20 MULTIPLE SALES OF TICKETS
Should the Licenser elect to sell a number of seats (a "block sale") to a particular individual or organization, at the request of the Hirer or otherwise, the Licenser shall determine in its absolute discretion the conditions relating to and the method of subsequent distribution or sale of tickets relating to the block sale.

The Licenser will, in its absolute discretion, require the tickets forming part of any multiple sale to carry the gross selling price of the ticket on the face of the ticket, and under no circumstances will the Licenser approve the deemed sale or onsale (to sell to a third party, i.e., ticketing agency) of a ticket unless this requirement is met.

6. Indemnities and Limitation of Liability

6.1 WARRANTY BY HIRER
The Hirer warrants that at the date of signing of this Agreement the Hirer has entered into a contract to stage the Event described in Item 2 of Schedule 1. If, prior to the date or dates for which the Center has been hired, such contract is terminated or rescinded or becomes unenforceable for any reasons whatsoever or the Licenser ascertains that a contract is or was not in existence, the Licenser shall not be obliged to hire the Center on the relevant date or dates to the Hirer and shall be free to enter into an agreement to hire the Center to any other person who has entered into a contract to stage a performance of the Event that the Hirer represented to the Licenser he/she was entitled to stage or alternatively to any person whatsoever.

6.2 HIRER INDEMNIFIES LICENSER
The Hirer hereby indemnifies the Licenser and agrees to keep the Licenser always indemnified in respect of all loss, damage, consequential loss, and damage, including but not limited to loss of profit directly or indirectly associated with the Hiring, claims by any person against the Licenser, and legal fees or consultant's fees that the Licenser may suffer or incur, and all moneys

that the Licenser may become liable to pay to any person in respect of or arising directly or indirectly out of the following:

i.   Any act, default, or omission on the part of the Hirer, its servants, agents,
     invitees, licensees, artists, and/or any Patrons;
ii. Any act, default, or omission on the part of any servant, agent, invitee, or
     licensee of the Licenser when acting under the direction, order, or control
     of the Hirer, its servants, agents, invitees, licensees, and artists or any
     Patrons at the Event;
iii. The Hirer not proceeding with the Hiring or any part thereof pursuant to
     this Agreement or canceling or postponing the Hiring or any part
     thereof; or
iv. The Hirer's failing to complete a contract made between the Hirer and a
     third party for the performance by the third party of work or services in
     connection with the Hiring, whether or not such contract is a contract
     under which the Licenser has agreed to keep the third party indemnified
     against loss, including loss of profit, occasioned by the Hirer's failing to
     complete such contract.
v.   Any claim for or breach of copyright, referred to in Clause 4.37;
vi. Performance of any work or works or exhibition that brings the Licenser,
     the Council, or the Center into disrepute;
vii. Any accident, damage, or injury to property in the Center or the grounds
     of the Center, any loss of property from the Center, any accident, dam-
     age, or injury to any person or to the property of any person suffered in or
     about the Center, the entrances, lobbies, and exits thereof, and the
     grounds surrounding the Center, where such accident, damage, injury, or
     loss arose by reason of, or in relation to, or in connection with the use of
     the Center or any part thereof by the Hirer, its servants, agents, invitees,
     or licensees or any Patron, except where such accident, damage, injury,
     or loss occurred by reason of the Licenser's sole negligence;
viii. Any interruption to or adverse effect upon any concurrent or future use of
     the Center or any part thereof by any other person; and
ix. The answers to any of the questions contained in the technical question-
     naire referred to in Clause 4.8 not being true and correct in all respects.
x.   Any loss, damage (including consequential loss or damage), claim pen-
     alty, fine, or charge suffered by or imposed on the Licenser directly or
     indirectly in consequence of any breach by the Hirer of its obligations
     pursuant to Clause 4.4 hereof or any failure on the part of the Hirer to
     otherwise comply with the provisions of the Workplace Health and
     Safety Act.

6.3 FORCE MAJEURE

The Licenser will not be liable to the Hirer, its servants, agents, subcontractors, invitees, licensees, players, performers, participants, exhibitors, or competitors for any loss or damage in respect of any liability howsoever arising that may be suffered or incurred by the Hirer, its servants, agents, invitees, or licensees or in respect of any goods or equipment owned, operated, or hired by the Hirer, its servants, agents, subcontractors, invitees or licensees, players, performers, participants, exhibitors, or competitors resulting from the following:

i.   Any strike or other industrial action by any person or group of persons, including, but not limited to, any employees or contractors engaged by or employed by the Licenser, its contractors, or the Hirer; or

ii. Any interruption or cessation in the supply of chilled water or electricity or any other type of power or energy to the Center or failure of any equipment owned or operated or hired by the Licenser for the supply of chilled water or electricity or any other power or energy to the Center; or

iii. Any decisions of the Licenser under Clause 8.1, any force majeure occurrence including acts of God; war, whether declared or undeclared, civil commotion, blockade, or insurrection; fire (including bush fire); flood or washaway; storm or tempest; smoke; bomb threats or other threats of violence or damage to person or property; earthquake; shortage of water; epidemic; explosion; serious breakage or accident to facility or equipment; an act or restraint of any governmental or semigovernmental or other public or statutory authority or any other cause not reasonably within the control of the Licenser, which may affect in whole or in part the Hiring and/or the obligations and/or liabilities of either party to this Agreement.

6.4 USE OF PREMISES AT HIRER'S RISK

The Hirer will use and occupy the Center and any part thereof at the risk of the Hirer, and this Agreement hereby releases to the full extent permitted by the law, the Council, the Licenser, and the servants, agents, invitees, and licensees of the Council, the Licenser and each of them from all liability howsoever arising resulting from the following:

i.   Any accident, loss, damage, or injury to persons or property occurring in the Center or any part thereof while occupied or used by the Hirer under the provisions of this Agreement; and

ii. Any loss or damage suffered by any person or persons arising out of the exercise by the Licenser of any right or discretion under this Agreement.

6.5 LICENSER NOT RESPONSIBLE FOR SELECTION OF WORKS

The rights and powers of the Licenser under this Agreement will not be deemed to impose upon the Licenser any responsibility or liability for the selection of the work or works proposed to be performed or being performed or the material or items proposed to be exhibited or being exhibited in the Center or any part thereof, and any granting, withholding, or refusal of any permission by the Licenser shall be construed accordingly, and the Hirer will ensure that no such work or works or exhibition will bring the Licenser, the Council, or the Center into disrepute.

6.6 LICENSER NOT RESPONSIBLE FOR ADEQUACY OF VENUE

The Licenser gives no warranty that the License Area will be adequate for and/or fit for the Hiring, and the Hirer agrees that it will satisfy itself as to such matters. The Licenser will not be liable to the Hirer for any loss or damage howsoever caused arising wholly or partially from the License Areas not being adequate and/or fit for the Hiring.

6.7 LICENSER NOT RESPONSIBLE FOR ADVICE, CONSENTS

The Hirer warrants that in the planning and presentation of the Event, including but not limited to the selection of the Center as a venue fit for or adequate for the Hiring, it has not and will not make any decisions solely reliant upon any professional advice or representation from the Licenser, its servants, agents, or employees. The Hirer will satisfy itself in relation to all matters regarding the presentation of the Event, and the Hirer shall in no respect be relieved of any of its obligations to the Licenser hereunder by reason of the fact that any such professional advice or representation shall have been given by the Licenser, its servants, agents, or employees to the Hirer, which shall be in contravention of any legislation, regulation, ordinance, or bylaw or shall be incorrect, insufficient, or misleading in any respect. Further, the Licenser will not be liable to the Hirer for any loss or damage howsoever caused arising wholly or partially from the reliance by the Hirer upon any such professional advice or representation. The Hirer acknowledges that where any consent or approval is granted by the Licenser or any inspection performed by the Licenser hereunder, the giving of such consent or approval or the making of such inspection shall in no respect make the Licenser liable to the Hirer for any loss or damage suffered (including consequential loss or damage) by the Hirer if the Hirer shall act in pursuance thereof, nor shall the granting of any such consent or approval or the making of any such inspection release the Hirer from any of its obligations hereunder.

6.8 LIABILITY OF LICENSER

The Hirer acknowledges that in dealing with the Licenser or any direction, servant, agent, or employee of the Licenser prior to the entering into of this Agreement or during the course of this Agreement, the Hirer is dealing with a corporation acting through its directors, servants, agents, or employees. The Hirer agrees to waive its rights with respect to any course of action available to it against any director, servant, agent, or employee of the Licenser in respect of any statement, representation, act, or omission of such director, servant, agent, or employee whether or not such statement, representation, act, or omission was authorized by the Licenser.

6.9 USE OF LICENSER'S EMPLOYEES.

The Hirer shall not be relieved from any liability, obligation, or duty to the Licenser hereunder or otherwise by reason only of the fact that such liability, obligation, or duty arose wholly or partly as a result of the acts or omissions of any employee of the Licenser if at such time the employee was acting or performing work on behalf of, for the benefit of, or under the direction or control of the Hirer.

7. Damage to the Center

7.1 DAMAGE BY HIRER

If the Center or its facilities or equipment is damaged by any act or omission, whether willful or otherwise, by the Hirer, its servants, agents, subcontractors, invitees, licensees, players, performers, participants, exhibitors, or competitors, any Patron, or by the Licenser's staff working at the direction of the Hirer under this Agreement or by any other person entering the Center pursuant to or in exercise of the rights granted by this Agreement to the Hirer, including a Patron attending a performance, the Hirer will pay to the Licenser and/or the Council on demand an amount equal to the costs incurred by the Licenser and/or the Council, as the case may be, in repairing and/or reinstating the damaged area, facilities, or equipment to the standard of repair and condition as such area, facilities, or equipment were in immediately prior to the Event *provided always* that if any equipment is damaged beyond repair, the Hirer shall pay to the Licenser the replacement cost of such equipment.

7.2 REPORT DAMAGE OR LOSS

The Hirer will advise the Licenser as soon as it becomes aware of damage or loss to the Center, its facilities, or equipment or any injury whatsoever to any person occurring in or about the Center in connection with the use of the Center or any part thereof, and the Hirer will deliver a copy of the full details of such occurrence to the Licenser as soon as practicable immediately following such occurrence.

8. Termination of License

8.1 TERMINATION BY LICENSER

In addition to any other right to terminate this Agreement that the Licenser may have hereunder or otherwise, if at any time the Licenser forms the opinion that:

i.   There is a real possibility that damage may be caused to the Center, its facilities, or its equipment by the Hirer exercising any right or authority granted pursuant to this Agreement or that such exercise may cause any injury to patrons or Licenser's staff or prejudice any agreement, maintenance contract or insurance policy of the Licenser;

ii. The manner in which any Hiring is being conducted or is proposed to be conducted is illegal or otherwise contrary to law or may injure or tend to injure the reputation of the Licenser, the Center, or the Council;

iii. There has been a material change after the date of signing of this Agreement to any items contained in the schedules or to any information provided by the Hirer prior to the signing of this Agreement;

iv. The Hirer is unable, upon demand, to provide documentation supporting his/her warranty pursuant to Clause 6.1;

v.   There exists an emergency in the Center, whether due to an actual or impending event, that has the effect of causing or threatening to cause loss of life or injury or distress to persons or danger to the safety of the public or any other persons or any part of the public or destruction or damage to property;

vi. The Center or any part thereof that substantially affects the Hiring is required, requisitioned, or resumed for the use of a government or local authority or any other public authority for any public purpose or priority usage by any government or local authority;

vii. The Center is damaged or destroyed by an act of war or in the course of resisting or repelling such action or is being repaired, remedied, or made good, or attempts are being made to do so as a result of such action;

viii. The use of the Center for the Hiring is prohibited, obstructed, or hindered by reason of the occurrence of any industrial action, strike, act of God, or civil disorder; or

ix. The Licenser's right to operate the Center expires or is terminated with or without fault on its part, or the Licenser is otherwise prevented by any mortgagee or creditor from performing this Agreement

the Licenser may terminate the License forthwith by notice to the Hirer.

8.2 EVENTS OF DEFAULT BY HIRER

If at any time:

i. Execution shall be levied against any of the assets of the Hirer or any guarantor of the Hirer's obligations under this Agreement

ii. The Hirer or any guarantor of the Hirer's obligations under this Agreement (not being a company) becomes bankrupt or assigns his/her estate or enters into a deed of arrangements for the benefit of creditors, or the Hirer or any guarantor of the Hirer's obligations under this Agreement (being a company) either

   a. Goes into liquidation (other than voluntary liquidation for the purposes of reorganization) or is wound up or dissolved,

   b. Enters into a scheme of arrangement with its creditors or any class thereof,

   c. Is placed under official management, or a receiver or manager of any of its assets is appointed, or

   d. Has an inspector appointed in respect of its affairs or certain of its affairs pursuant to the Companies Code, or any equivalent legislation

the Licenser may terminate the License forthwith by notice to the Hirer.

8.3 SUBSTANTIAL BREACH

If at any time there has been a substantial breach of any obligation of the Hirer pursuant to this Agreement or if in the opinion of the Licenser the organization or advertising for or the manner in which any Hiring is being conducted or is proposed to be conducted is likely to be scandalous, libelous, obscene, or of an objectionable character, then the Licenser may terminate the License forthwith by notice to the Hirer.

8.4 NOTICE OF TERMINATION

Any notice of termination given pursuant to this Clause 8 shall be given in the manner provided in Clause 11. Such notice may be conditional on any matter specified therein and shall take effect in accordance with its tenor.

8.5 CONSEQUENCES OF TERMINATION

In the event that the Licenser gives notice pursuant to Subclauses 8.1 or 8.2, such notice will take effect without prejudice to the rights or remedies that the Licenser would have had but for the said notice in respect of or arising out of any antecedent breach of the Agreement by the Hirer.

8.6 LICENSER TO DEDUCT SUMS PAID OR PAYABLE

In the event that the License is terminated pursuant to Clauses 8.1.i to 8.1.iv, or 8.2, the Licenser will be entitled, in addition to any other rights that may be conferred upon it at law or in equity, to retain any Security Deposit paid hereunder. Additionally, the Licenser will be entitled to retain or sue for as a debt all sums paid or payable pursuant to this Agreement before the date of the termination and also to deduct same from the Security Deposit or any Box Office moneys due and payable to the Hirer.

8.7 INTEREST ON OVERDUE MONEYS

In the event of default by the Hirer in the due payment of any amount payable under this Agreement, the Hirer shall pay interest on the amount in respect of which such default is made from the date of such default until the date of actual payment at a rate of interest equal to the prevailing prime rate [*Author's note*: specify reference for prime rate, e.g., Money Rate Section of *The Wall Street Journal* on a specified date] for ninety (90) days commercial bills for each month or part of a month during which any such payment shall be overdue. If the liability of the Hirer to pay such amount shall become merged in any judgment or order of any Court, the Hirer shall pay interest on the amount for the time being owing under such judgment or order from the date that such judgment or orders takes effect until the date of actual payment or recovery at the aforesaid rate.

8.8 HIRER'S DISCHARGE

In the Event that the License is terminated solely pursuant to Clause 8.1.v through 8.1.ix and the Hirer is not responsible in any way whatsoever for any Event referred to in such Clause, the Licenser will refund any Security Deposit or Deposits paid by the Hirer pursuant to this Agreement. Receipt by the Hirer for the amount of such Security Deposit or Deposits shall be a full discharge and satisfaction of all Hirer's claims against the Licenser pursuant to this Agreement.

9. Licenser's Undertakings

9.1 LICENSER TO MAKE FACILITIES AVAILABLE

The Licenser will make all reasonable efforts to make available for the Hirer's use such facilities, equipment, and/or services of the Center as are required by the Hirer *provided always* that the Licenser makes no warranty and accepts no responsibility for the adequacy or suitability of such facilities, equipment, and/or services for the particular Event and that the Hirer will rely solely upon his/her own estimation of such adequacy and suitability.

9.2 LICENSER TO ALLOW HIRER ACCESS

The Licenser will allow the Hirer, its servants, agents, invitees, and licensees access to all parts of the Center other than the License Area that are necessarily used in connection with the Hiring at any time during the continuance of the License *provided always* that access shall not include those parts of the Center used by the Licenser's administration, the plant room, computer control rooms, box office, board room, private lounges, service tunnels, machinery lofts, and the roof of the Center or any catering or merchandise stores or any other storage areas or areas of the Center whatsoever other than the License Area and its immediate and associated service and facilities areas unless otherwise agreed by the Licenser.

10. Assignment

10.1 NO HIRER'S ASSIGNMENT

The Hirer will not be entitled to assign its interest and obligations under this Agreement without the prior written consent of the Licenser, which consent may be given or withheld in the Licenser's absolute discretion.

10.2 LICENSER'S ASSIGNMENT

The Licenser will be entitled, without the consent of the Hirer, to assign its interest and obligations under this Agreement to any party that by reason of assignment, appointment, or any other reason whatsoever replaces it as the manager under the management agreement.

11. Notices

11.1 WRITTEN COMMUNICATION

Any notice, communication, or other document authorized or required to be given or served pursuant to this Agreement (hereinafter referred to as a "communication") will, unless otherwise specifically provided by this Agreement, be in writing addressed as appropriate to the relevant party at its address set out in this Clause 11.4 or to such other address as may be notified in writing by that party to the other party hereto from time to time as its address for service hereunder and will be signed by a duly authorized officer of the party giving or serving the communication.

11.2 COMMUNICATION

A communication will be delivered by hand or sent by telex or facsimile transmission or by mail.

11.3 TELEX OR FACSIMILE COMMUNICATION

A communication that is delivered by hand or sent by facsimile transmission before 5:00 P.M. on a business day in the place of delivery shall be deemed to be received on that day and in all other cases shall be deemed to be received on the following business day in the place of delivery, and communication that is sent by telex shall be deemed to be received on receipt by the machine on which that telex is transmitted at the end of such transmission of the answer-back code of the party to whom it was sent if that receipt occurs before 5:00 P.M. on a business day in the place of receipt and in all other cases shall be deemed to be received on the following business day in the place of receipt *provided that* this Clause will not operate when the transmission is not intelligible. Transmission will be deemed to have been fully intelligible unless the transmission is requested within two (2) working hcurs (being hours between 9:00 A.M. and 5:00 P.M. on a weekday) from the ti. ie the communication was received. A communication sent by mail will be deemed to be received forty-eight (48) hours after the time of the postmark.

11.4 ADDRESS OF LICENSER

The address and facsimile transmission number of the Licenser are as follows:

    Address _____
    Facsimile number _____

11.5 ADDRESS OF HIRER

The address and facsimile transmission number (if any) of the Hirer is as specified in Item 10 of Schedule 1.

11.6 DELIVERY TO NOMINEE

Notwithstanding the foregoing provisions of this Clause 11, a communication will be deemed to have been duly given and/or served if it is signed by and/or hand delivered to the Licenser's nominee or the Hirer's nominee, as the case may be, appointed pursuant to Clause 12.4 or 12.5, respectively.

12. Miscellaneous Provisions

12.1 WAIVER

This Agreement and the rights and obligations expressed herein will not be abrogated, prejudiced, or affected by the granting of time, credit, or any indulgence or concession by the Licenser to the Hirer or to any other person whomsoever or by any compounding, compromise, release, abandonment, waiver, variation, relinquishment, or renewal of any rights of the Licenser or by any omission or neglect or any other dealing, matter, or thing that but for this Clause could or might operate to abrogate, prejudice, or affect the rights of the Licenser or the obligation of the Hirer, and failure of the Licenser to exercise any of its rights in respect of any breach of this Agreement will not operate as a waiver of any of its rights arising hereunder, and waiver of one or more of the terms and conditions and undertakings herein will not operate as a variation of this Agreement. Time will be of the essence of all obligations under this Agreement.

12.2 ARBITRATION

If any dispute, question, or difference will arise between the parties as to the effect of any statement, representation, act, or omission made by the Licenser prior to the entering into of this Agreement or in the course of this Agreement as to the meaning, operation, or effect of this Agreement or as to the rights or liabilities of either of the parties hereto, such dispute, question, or difference will be referred to arbitration by a single arbitrator or such other person as for the purpose of appointing an arbitrator whose decision or award will be conclusive and binding on the parties, and any such submission to arbitration shall be deemed to be a submission to arbitration with the meanings of the Arbitration Act (1973), and subject to the provisions of that Act an award pursuant to a reference to arbitration in accordance with this provision will be a condition precedent to any action or other legal proceeding between the parties relating to such dispute, question, or difference.

12.3 LICENSEE'S CAPACITY

The Hirer hereby represents and warrants to the Licenser that the Hirer has as at the date hereof and shall throughout the Hiring have sufficient assets to enable it to discharge all of its obligations hereunder in addition to meeting all other liabilities (whether actual or contingent) that it may owe or for which it may be liable from time to time.

12.4 LICENSER'S NOMINEE

The signatory to this Agreement on behalf of the Licenser will also be the Licenser's nominee, but in the instance that the Licenser decides to appoint another Licenser's nominee, the Licenser will notify the Hirer of the said appointment. Any approval, determination, notice, consent, or other right to be given, made, or exercised by the Licenser under this Agreement may be given, made, or exercised by the Licenser's nominee on its behalf, and the Hirer will be entitled to rely on any act done by the Licenser's nominee as binding on the Licenser.

12.5 HIRER'S NOMINEE

The Hirer will appoint a Hirer's nominee and shall notify the Licenser of such appointment. The Hirer shall ensure that the Hirer's nominee is present in the Center or available at all times during the Hiring. The Licenser and the Licenser's nominee will be entitled to rely on any act done by the Hirer's nominee as binding on the Hirer.

12.6 GOVERNING LAW

This Agreement will be governed and construed with reference to the laws of the State notwithstanding the principles, if any, that would otherwise govern the choice of the applicable law in the absence of the parties' selection of the laws of the State. Each of the parties hereto submits to the jurisdiction of the courts in conjunction with its determination of the rights and remedies of either of the parties hereto under this Agreement.

12.7 GUARANTEE

If requested by the Licenser, the Hirer will procure the execution of the guarantee and indemnify in the form hereunder or such other form as the Licenser may require by such person or corporation as the Licenser may require. If requested by the Licenser, the Hirer will furnish a bank guarantee in a form satisfactory to the Licenser.

GUARANTEE AND INDEMNITY (Attachment to Hiring Agreement)

In consideration of the Licenser at the request of (Name of Guarantor) (hereinafter called "the Guarantor," which expression shall mean and include the said person or corporation and its respective executors, administrators, successors, and assignees) entering into the attached Hiring Agreement ("the Agreement") with the Hirer, the Guarantor agrees with the Licenser that:

i. The Guarantor guarantees to the Licenser that the Guarantor will be jointly and severally liable with the Hirer to the Licenser for the due payment of all moneys to be paid by the Hirer under the Agreement and the due performance and observance by the Hirer of all the terms and conditions of the Agreement on the part of the Hirer to be performed and observed.

ii. The Guarantor will indemnify the Licenser and agrees at all times hereafter to keep the Licenser indemnified from and against all losses and expenses that the Licenser may suffer or incur in consequence of any breach or nonobservance of any of the terms and conditions of the Agreement on the part of the Hirer to be performed or observed, and the Guarantor agrees that the Guarantor shall remain liable to the Licenser under this indemnity notwithstanding that as a consequence of such breach or nonobservance that the Licenser has exercised any of its rights under the Agreement including its rights of termination and notwithstanding that the Hirer (being a company) may be wound up or dissolved or being a natural person may be declared bankrupt and notwithstanding that this guarantee may for any reasons whatsoever be unenforceable either in whole or in part.

iii. On any default or failure by the Hirer to observe and perform any of the terms and conditions of the Agreement, the Guarantor will forthwith on demand pay all moneys payable to the Licenser under the Agreement and make good to the Licenser all losses and expenses sustained or incurred by the Licenser by reason or in consequence of any such default or failure by the Hirer in the payment of moneys or in performing or observing any of the terms and conditions of the Agreement without the necessity of any prior demand having been made on the Hirer.

iv. The liability of the Guarantor under this guarantee and indemnity shall not be affected by the granting of time or any other indulgence to or by the compounding, compromise, release, abandonment, waiver, variation, or renewal of any of the rights of the Licenser against the Hirer or by any neglect or omission to enforce such rights or by any other thing which under the law relating to sureties would or might but for this provision release the Guarantor in whole or in part from the Guarantor's obligations under this guarantee.

v. Notwithstanding that as between the Guarantor and the Hirer the Guarantor may be a surety only nevertheless that as between the Guarantor and the Licenser, the Guarantor shall be deemed to be a primary debtor and contractor jointly and severally with the Hirer.

vi. To the fullest extent permitted by law the Guarantor hereby waives such of his/her rights as surety or indemnifier (legal, equitable, statutory, or otherwise) that may at any time be inconsistent with any of the provisions of the guarantee and indemnity contained in the Agreement.

vii. The covenants and agreements made or given by the Guarantor shall not be conditional or contingent in any way or dependent on the validity or enforceability of the covenants and agreements of any other person and shall be and remain binding notwithstanding that any other person shall not have executed or duly executed the Agreement or this guarantee and indemnity.

viii. The obligations of the Guarantor under this guarantee and indemnity shall continue to remain in force until all license fees or other moneys payable pursuant to the Agreement have been paid and until all other obligations and indemnities shall have been performed and satisfied and such obligation shall not be reduced or affected by notice of termination or rescission given by either party to the Agreement or the mental illness, death, insolvency, liquidation, or dissolution of the Hirer.

ix. If the Guarantor includes more than one person or corporation in the obligations under this guarantee, indemnity shall bind every two or more such persons or corporations jointly and each of them severally.

12.8 SEVERABILITY

The invalidity or illegality of any part of this Agreement will not, if the Licenser so elects, affect the validity or force of any other part of this Agreement.

12.9 NO PARTNERSHIP, JOINT VENTURE, AGENCY, OR LEASE

Nothing in this Agreement will be deemed or construed by the parties or any third party as creating the relationship of partnership, joint venture, or principal and agent between the Licenser and the Hirer or as granting to the Hirer a lease of the Center.

12.10 AUTHORITY OF SIGNING PARTIES

Each signing party personally warrants that it has due authority to sign this Agreement and that such authority has not and will not be revoked during the currency of this Agreement.

12.11 ENTIRE AGREEMENT

Notwithstanding anything said or written prior to the signing hereof by the parties or their authorized representatives, this Agreement embodies the entire understanding of the parties and constitutes the entire terms agreed upon between the parties hereto and supersedes any prior agreement between the parties on the subject matter hereof, and there are no promises, terms, conditions, or obligations, oral or written, expressed, or implied, other than those contained herein, except to the extent that any term, condition, or obligation implied by law is at law not able to be excluded.

12.12 VARIATION

No variation, waiver, or modification of any of the terms of this Agreement shall be valid unless in writing and signed by the authorized representatives of the parties hereto.

12.13 PRIOR CONDITIONS

Notwithstanding anything herein contained or any communication whether written or oral whether prior to, on, or after the date hereof, this contract shall not become binding on the Licenser until the occurrence of the last to occur of the following events:

12.13.1. The execution hereof by or on behalf of the Hirer.

12.13.2. The execution hereof by the Licenser and the banking by the Licenser of the Security Deposit and, if it is paid by check, the clearance of the check.

In witness whereof the parties hereto have executed this Agreement made on the _____ day of 19___

_____

Signed for and on behalf of the Hirer in the presence of

_____

Witness Name of Signatory

_____

Date

_____

_____

_____

Name and Address of Witness, Position of Hirer (printed)

_____

Signed for and on behalf of the Licenser in the presence of

_____

Witness Name of Signatory

_____

Date

_____

_____

_____

Name and Address of Witness, Position with Licenser (printed)

INDEMNITY (ATTACHMENT TO HIRING AGREEMENT)

Whereas:

A. "The Council" is the owner of the Center referred to in the attached Hiring Agreement.

B. It is a condition of the Council consenting to the Licensees entering into the attached Agreement that this indemnity be executed by the Hirer referred to therein.

Now the Hirer covenants and agrees with the Council as follows:

The Hirer hereby indemnifies the Council and agrees to keep the Council always indemnified in respect of all actions, suits, claims, costs, charges, expenses, demands, and other liabilities whatsoever that the Council may suffer made by any person (including the Hirer) in respect of any personal injury and/or death and/or damage to property and/or consequential loss and/or pecuniary loss or other losses, damages, or liabilities whatsoever arising out of or in any way connected with the Hiring referred to in the attached Hiring Agreement, and without limiting the generality of the foregoing, the Hirer indemnifies the Council as follows:

1. Whether the foregoing involve any act, default, or submission on the part of the Council or the Licenser or their respective servants, agents, invitees, licensees, or others;

2. Against the foregoing in respect of claims in respect of breach of copyright, performing right, or other protected right, or performance of any work or works or exhibition that brings the Council or the Center into disrepute;

3. Against the foregoing in respect of any accident, damage, injury to property in the Center or the grounds of the Center and any accident, damage,

or injury to any person or to the property of any person suffered in or about the Center where such accident, damage, injury, or loss arises by reason of or in relation to or in connection with the Hiring.

Signed, sealed, and delivered by for and on behalf of the Hirer in the presence of

---

SCHEDULE 1

ITEM 1

Hirer

ITEM 2

Hiring

ITEM 3

License area: Main arena

ITEM 4

License period: From 6:00 A.M., Wednesday, 25th September 1996, until 6:00 A.M., Thursday, 26th September 1996

ITEM 5

Time by which Hirer must be clear of Center at end of license period: 6:00 A.M., Thursday, 26th September 1996

ITEM 6

Starting time: To be advised

Intermission time: To be advised

Finishing time: To be advised

ITEM 7

Merchandising terms: Commission 17.5 percent of gross sales plus reimbursement of costs, including wages.

ITEM 8

Proposed ticket prices: To be compiled by Hirer

ITEM 9

Proposed ticket on-sale date: To be completed by Hirer

ITEM 10

Hirer's address:

Telephone:

Facsimile transmission number:

SCHEDULE 2

PART A

1. License Charge

Item: Wednesday, 25th September 1996

Charge: 15 percent of Gross Box Office Proceeds with a minimum guarantee of $5000.00 (five thousand dollars) per performance and with a minimum guarantee of $5000.00 (five thousand dollars) per scheduled performance date not used, plus costs

2. Additional Amounts and Costs to Be Charged Against Hirer

Licenser's staff costs

Additional staff costs

Licenser's subcontractors' costs

Booking fees

Credit/debit card charges

Catering requirements of hirer

Cleaning and waste disposal charges

Electricity charges

Technical and production costs

Follow spot hire

Installation or hire of additional equipment

Lamp replacement cost

Telephone and fax usage

Damage restitution

Public risk insurance

Cost of any insurance taken out by the Licenser upon default by Hirer in its obligations under Subclause 4.33 of this Agreement

Any costs incurred by the Licenser pursuant to Clause 9.1 that are not otherwise specified in this Schedule

Any costs of further requirements by hirer

Any other amounts, costs, or expenses reasonably incurred by the Licenser or owed to the Licenser by the Hirer, whether incurred in respect of the License hereby granted and/or the Hiring or otherwise

If applicable, the Hirer agrees to pay to the Licenser an industrial relations service fee on a per performance basis on the scale of rates as apply on the date of the performance or performances, such rates being established from time to time by the executive council of the Entertainment Industry Employers Association.

PART B

Security Deposit: $5000.00 (five thousand dollars), payable upon execution of the Agreement or by the 1st April 1996.

SCHEDULE 3

ITEM 1

Council area/seats: Twenty-four seats (24) per performance

ITEM 2

Licenser's area/seats (for approved sale): Three hundred seats (300) per performance

ITEM 3

Licenser's area/seats (house seats): One hundred seats (100) per performance

ITEM 4

Hirer's area/seats: To be advised

SCHEDULE 4

[Variations to standard form agreement, if any.]

SCHEDULE 5

Box PLAN

Please indicate on the Box Plan the precise location and dimensions of the proposed stage or performance area; indicate the location and dimensions of any equipment that may obstruct the full and clear sightlines of the Event for a Patron; and indicate the seating areas that the Hirer warrants will have full and clear sightlines of the Event. This information is required before any tickets for the Event are distributed or released for sale.

SCHEDULE 6

Advertising, Publicity, and Promotion Information

1. NAME OF CENTER

The Center will be referred to only as "The Entertainment Center."

2. TICKET PRICES

Gross Ticket Prices (inclusive of the $1.80 System Booking Fee, payable by the Hirer) will be included in all advertising.

An Outlet Service Fee (currently $2.00 per ticket) will be charged to a customer at an agency for the convenience of the remote agency, and a Service Fee (currently $2.00 per ticket) will be charged to a customer for credit card, taxes, and mail bookings. These service fees are subject to review from time to time.

No agency fee will be charged to a customer purchasing a ticket for an Event at the Center from the Box Office at the Center.

Therefore ticket prices will be advertised as "$(Gross Price) plus agency fee when applicable," and ticket prices will be included in advertising when applicable for the convenience of prospective patrons.

Tickets pulled for the Hirer as "complimentary" or "no charge" will attract a 20 cents fee to cover costs.

Complimentary tickets may be overstamped prior to supply with the words "Complimentary—Not for Resale" or similar.

3. EVENT TIMES

The Event commencement time, as detailed in this Agreement, will be included in each advertisement.

4. SUPPORTING ACTS

When applicable, the supporting act for the Event will be included in each advertisement.

5. BOX OFFICE LOCATIONS

Box Office locations for inclusion in all advertising will be as follows:

Tickets available at the Center, on the mall, and all outlets.

6. BOX OFFICE TRADING HOURS

The Entertainment Center Box Office trading hours will be as follows:

Monday through Friday	9:00 A.M. to 5:00 P.M.
Saturday	9:00 A.M. to 12 P.M.

All outlets operate normal retail trading hours as applicable to their location. Telephone bookings and the group booking office will also operate as follows:

Monday through Friday	9:00 A.M. to 5:00 P.M.
Saturday	9:00 A.M. to 12 P.M.

The release time for tickets for a new Event will be 9:05 A.M. on the relevant day.

7. TELEPHONE CREDIT CARD BOOKINGS

Telephone credit card bookings will be available and advertised as follows:

555–555–5555

8. EVENT INQUIRIES TELEPHONE

As an additional service to the public, an 800-line Event Inquiries Telephone Service has been established and will be advertised as follows:

Event Inquiries 1–800–555–5555

9. GROUP BOOKINGS

Groups of 20 or more can book by telephoning the Group Bookings Line, and, when applicable, this service will be advertised as follows:

Group Bookings (20 or more), phone Melissa at 555–555–5555

10. CREDIT CARD BOOKING REQUESTS BY FAX

Credit card booking requests will be accepted by fax, which should be advertised as follows:

555–555–5555

11. MAIL BOOKINGS

When applicable, mail bookings will be advertised as follows:

Mail details of ticket requirements to
"Event Title"

c/o _____

Make check payable to "Payee"

Include a stamped, self-addressed envelope for return of tickets.

12. MAIL BOOKINGS COUPONS

When applicable, mail booking coupons will be included in print media advertising, and layout will be approved by Licenser prior to publishing.

13. DOOR SALES

Subject to availability, tickets for an Event will be available at the door 90 minutes prior to commencement of the Event.

14. WEEKENDS AND PUBLIC HOLIDAYS

Special arrangements may be made for ticket sales on weekends and public holidays, and the relative details supplied by the Licenser will be included in that day's advertising.

15. PROGRAM

When a program for the Event is to be printed, the Hirer will submit to the Licenser for approval details relating to the Licenser or the Center.

SCHEDULE 7

Technical Questionnaire

Pursuant to the terms of the Hiring Agreement, please complete the following details in full, as this information is essential to the Agreement and will assist the Entertainment Center in scheduling your Event in the most cost-efficient manner. It is understood that there may be insufficient space on this form to accommodate the fullest possible declaration of information and requirements. In this instance please attach details of any further information available.

N.B. It is the Hirer's responsibility to ensure that any equipment or structure utilized in connection with the Event has received the appropriate approvals required by state law, that any relevant inspections are completed, and that any required certificates, licenses, or documentation are current and available at all times during the Hiring for inspection by any government department or by the Center.

1. Production:
2. Production company:
        Contact:
        Status:
        Telephone number:

3. Load in:
    Date:
    Time:
    Load out:
    Date:
    Estimated time of completion:
4. Number of semitrailers arriving:
5. Other vehicles, including caravans (please specify):
6. Number of artists or competitors:
    Number of touring crew:
    Number of casual crew:
    Support act name:
    Support act number:
7. Mode:
    Concert mode   Corner Mode   Intimate mode   Reduced concert mode
    Arena mode   Other (State number of seats required)
8. Dressing room allocation

Room 1:	Room 2:	Room 3:
Room 4:	Room 5:	Room 6:
Room 7: Production	Room 8:	Room 9:
Room 10:	Room 11:	Room 12:
Blue room:	Chorus room:	Musicians' room:
Glass office:		

9. Technical staff

    Electrician: Yes/No   Number required: Call time:
    Riggers: Yes/No   Number required: Call time:
10. Number of rigging points:
    Sound system
    Lighting
    Other

    Please provide a detailed scale plan of all points indicating position, dead weight, live loads, moving truss, and so on.
11. Stage
    Size:
    Height:
    Wings (sound):
    Distance from back wall:
    Weight onstage:

    (The stock stage is built of modules 2.4 m by 1.8 m and can vary in height from 1.2 m to 1.8 m at 200-mm intervals).

    Please note: There is a charge for erection of the stage.

Crash barrier: Yes/No

Stock/Other:

12. Power to the stage

Power available: 1200 amps/3 phase, 3 phase neutral and earth. (Single insulated main cables must not be used in this Center.)

Portable generator unit:

Fumes (internal/external):

Fire extinguisher (size):

Other:

13. Follow spots

The Entertainment Center has four 2000 watt XEBEX follow spots, available for hire at $70 each for the first performance of a hiring and then $35 each for every performance thereafter.

Entertainment Center house spots: Yes/No

If yes, how many:

Total number of spots required: FOH: Truss:

Call times:

14. Other lighting requirements

The Entertainment Center has 1000 narrow-beam par cans and 30 sports floods.

Do you require the use of par cans? Yes/No

If yes, please provide details regarding position, color, and so on.

Sports floods: Yes/No

If yes, please provide details (i.e., position, television requirements, and so on).

The sports floods are nondimmable and do require a 30-minute start time and 30 minutes' cooling time before a restart.

Note: There is a labor charge for the positioning, patching, coloring, focusing, plotting of any of the Entertainment Center lights and a charge of $0.03 per par can per hour and $30 per performance for sports floods.

15. Audio

Do you require the house public address system? Yes/No

If yes, please provide details of your requirements.

If no, please advise the name of the audio contractor or subcontractor.

16. Talk-back facilities

Do you require the house talk system? Yes/No

If yes, please provide details of station numbers, position, and stage manager operator.

17. Videotaping

Do you require the following:

Fixed camera or cameras in the main arena? Yes/No

Closed-circuit television control room? Yes/No

Split of audio from house public address system? Yes/No

Video hardware? Yes/No

If yes to any or all of the above, please provide full details of your requirements.

18. Pyrotechnics

If you wish to use any pyrotechnic or firearm devices at the Center, please provide:

    a.   Documentation from the MFD (Metropolitan Fire Department) and City Council. All laid-out conditions must be adhered to for departmental inspection check.

    b.   A copy, by the first day of fit up of a current explosives license, to the Center.

Explosive license and valid certificate must be signed by commencement of load in.

Failure to comply with the above may prohibit the use of the Hirer's pyrotechnics and firearms.

If you wish to use smoke-producing equipment, the Hirer must advise the Center of its scheduled usage so the smoke detectors in the area can be isolated.

Fireboard operator is required during the day if isolation is required.

Failure to advise the Center will result in a call to the fire department, the charge for which will be payable by the Hirer.

19. Special effects

Provide details of any special elements, such as flying effects, lasers, quad sound, water jets or fountains, being used within the Center.

20. Further requirements

Please advise if any of the following is required for your Event:

    Basketball court: Yes/No

    Private boxes, number and configuration: Yes/No

    Grandstand removed totally: Yes/No

    Grandstand removed partially: Yes/No

    Tennis court or courts: Yes/No

    Flat floor, no stage: Yes/No

    Altering surface of floor: Yes/No

    Ice floor and depth: Yes/No

    Boxing ring: Yes/No

    Exhibition hall: Yes/No

    Telephones, power, etc., for Exhibition Hall: Yes/No

If answering yes to any of the above, please send detailed information and plans to the Center.

21. Please furnish full and accurate details of any further technical or production requirements and details of any information of which the Center should be made aware.

Please also detail in writing any information that the Hirer requires from the Center.

Your ability to furnish complete details through this Technical Questionnaire will assist the Hirer and the Entertainment Center in assisting to stage a successful and safe event.

TRANSLATIONS OF COMMON TERMS

English	Japanese	French	German
Stage left	Kamite	Scène gauche	Buhne links
Stage right	Shimote	Scène droite	Buhne rechts
Upstage	Butai oku	Au fond de la scène	Auf der Buhne
Downstage	Butai mae	Le devant de la scène	Unter den Buhne
Houselights	Cak den	Eclairage de la salle	Hause Licht
Paging system	Gakuya hohsch	Service de liason	Kontakt System
Water	Mizu	L'eau	Wasser
Sound/PA	Onkyoh	Son/PA	Ton
Lights	Lites	Lumières	Licht
Intermission, interval	Kyuh-kei	Entr'acte	Pause

GLOSSARY

absorption   Damping of a sound wave passing through a medium or striking a surface. The property of materials, objects, or media to absorb sound energy.

AC   Abbreviation for *alternating current*.

acoustics   The science of sound. The factors that determine the quality of received sound in a room or auditorium.

ad lib   To cover an unexpected situation in a show or hide a lapse of memory.

alignment   The process of setting controls and functions for optimum system performance.

ambiance   The combination of reverberation and background noise that characterizes the sound of a given room.

ampere   The common unit of current; the rate of flow of electricity.

amplifier   An electronic device for magnifying electrical signals to a level to which speakers respond.

amplitude   The peak of a sound waveform.

analog   Electronic signal the waveform of which resembles that of the original signal, as opposed to digital.

anechoic   Without echo. The walls of an anechoic chamber are lined with a material that completely absorbs any sound.

arc light   A lamp in which a carbon-arc discharge is the source of illumination.

arena   A venue where the audience is seated to the sides of the stage as well as the front.

attack time   The time taken for the onset of gain reduction in a compressor.

attenuation   The reduction of level at the source.

auto transformer   An iron-cored coil across an AC supply that allows various voltages to be selected.

azimuth   The angle between the gap of a tape head and the tape.

baffle   General term for a wall, board, or enclosure that carries a speaker. The baffle separates the front and back radiations from the speaker because they would otherwise cancel out each other.

balanced line   Program cable in which twin signal wires are both isolated from the earth.

bandwidth   The interval between cutoff frequencies.

barndoors   A metal fitting attached to the front of a floodlight that allows the light to be cut off by two or four hinged flaps.

base   The part of a lamp to which the electrical connection is made. Also the mechanical support of the lamp.

bass   Low-frequency end of the audio spectrum.

bass reflex   Type of speaker cabinet with an outlet (port) that allows enclosed air to improve the efficiency at low frequencies. This phenomenon is caused by the inversion of phase within the enclosure so that the radiations from the port aid the radiations from the cone.

batten   A length of rigid material hung on spot lines in a theater.

beam   The cone of light from a lighting instrument.

beam light   A light with no lens that gives a parallel beam.

black light   Ultraviolet light.

boom   Vertical pipe for hanging lamps. An extendible arm on a microphone stand for supporting microphones.

border   An abbreviated drop. Used for masking trusses and fly bars.

break jack   A jack arranged to break the normal circuit when a plug is inserted.

bridle   The wire ropes that attach to chain motors to achieve the correct rigging position using available rigging points.

bulb   The glass or quartz part of a lamp that encloses the filament or electrodes.

bus bar   Common earth or other contact wire.

cans   Headphones.

carbon arc   Light created by the gaseous discharge between two cerium-cored carbon rods. These rods burn for a limited time; an operator must maintain the intensity and sharpness of the light.

cardiod microphone   A microphone with a heart-shaped directivity pattern.

channel   Sequence of circuits or components that handle one specific signal.

circuit breaker   A device used instead of a fuse to open a circuit automatically when it is overloaded.

clamps, C and G   Devices used to attach lamps to pipes or trusses. So called because of their shape.

clipping   Distortion in a mixer or amplifier due to severe overloading.

compression   The process of reducing dynamic range. A compressed signal has a higher dynamic range.

compressor   A variable-gain amplifier in which the gain is controlled by the input signal, used to reduce dynamic range.

concert pitch   System of tuning music based on a frequency of A = 440 Hz.

condenser microphone   Type of microphone in which the signal is generated by the variation of capacitance between the diaphragm and a fixed plate.

counterweight system   A mechanical system for flying lamps, drapes, and scenery with a counterweight that runs up and down a track at the side of the stage.

crossfade   To fade in one channel while fading out another.

crossover   A unit for dividing the signal into separate frequency bands.

crossover frequency   The transition frequency at which the crossover splits the signal.

crosstalk   Unwanted breakthrough from adjacent channels.

cue   A point at which certain adjustments are required during a performance.

cue sheet   A record of the scenes and changes for each segment of the show.

curtain   A drape that hides the stage from the audience.

cyc light   A light fitting with a specially shaped reflector that produces a broad, elongated light beam enabling a cyclorama to be lit evenly overall from a relatively close distance.

cyclorama   A stretch of taut vertical cloth used as a general-purpose scenic background. Also called *eye*.

damping   Process of reducing unwanted resonant effects by applying absorbant material to a speaker cabinet. Poor damping allows the motion of the speaker to continue once the signal has been removed, creating a booming sound that masks the clarity.

DC   Abbreviation for *direct current*. It flows in one direction only, unlike AC.

decay time   The recovery time of a compressor or other processing device for the circuit to return to normal once the signal has been removed.

decibel   One decibel (dB) is the smallest change in loudness that the average human ear can detect. Zero decibels is the threshold of human hearing. The threshold of pain is between 120 and 130 dB. The decibel is a ratio, not an absolute number, and is used to identify the relation among true power, voltage, and sound pressure levels. Decibels alone have no specific meaning. For example, dB V is a voltage ratio; 0 dB = 0.775 V root mean square (RMS). dB SPL is the sound-pressure level ratio. It measures acoustic pressure. dBM is a power ratio. dBA takes into account the unequal sensitivity of the ear, and sound pressure level is measured through a circuit that compensates for this equal loudness. These measurements are termed *A weighted*.

diffraction   The manner in which sound can bend around obstacles.

diffuser   Translucent material used in front of lamps to soften and disperse the light quality and reduce the intensity.

digital sound   The process of converting a normal analog signal into a series of numerical measurements that can be transmitted as a digital code.

dimmer   An electrical circuit used to regulate the current flowing through the lamps to which it is connected, allowing adjustments in lighting intensity.

direct injection   The process of feeding an electronic musical instrument directly into the control console instead of through a microphone.

dispersion   The extent to which light rays or sound waves are scattered or diffused.

downstage   A position at the front of the stage closest to the audience.

drop   A cloth suspended from fly bars or grid to mask the stage, also called a *backdrop*.

dynamic range   The range of signal levels from lowest to highest. A program with wide dynamic range has a large variation between the loudest and quietest parts.

echo   Sound that has been reflected and arrives with such a magnitude and time interval after the direct sound as to be a distinguishable repeat of the original.

ellipsoidal spotlight   A spotlight in which the light collected from an ellipsoidal reflector (mirror) is focused on a lens. The shape of the light beam is adjustable by an internal variable iris, silhouette stencil (gobo), or independent framing shutters. Most of these lamps are designed to project perforated metal gobos.

EPROM   Acronym for *erasable programmable read only memory.*

equalization   The process of modifying the amplitude and frequency response to produce flat overall response, minimize noise, or create an artistic effect.

expander   An amplifier that increases gain as the input level increases, a characteristic that stretches dynamic range.

feedback   Signal from the output of system returns to the input producing unwanted oscillation that can quickly become out of control and cause severe damage to speaker components.

flash through   A check of the lighting system one channel at a time.

flat   A unit section of scenery. A tall screen.

flies   The space above the stage occupied by sets of lines, hanging drapes, and lamps.

flood   A type of light fitting that illuminates a wide area.

fluorescent lamp   A tubular lamp in which a mercury vapor discharge energizes a fluorescent powder coating on the inside of the tube.

fly   To lift equipment above the stage with electrical chain hoists or on a counterweight system.

focus   To position the lamps so that the beams light the desired areas.

FOH   Abbreviation for *front of house*; the front of an auditorium, opposite the stage.

foldback   Signals returning from the house console to the stage. Foldback becomes a monitor system when a separate console is used to control the onstage monitors.

follow spot   High-intensity lamp that requires an operator to follow the subject being lit and control the intensity and color.

frammel   A strip of wood placed between speaker cabinets to separate and angle them vertically to reduce phase interference between cabinets.

frequency   The rate of repetition of signal, measured in hertz (Hz).

Fresnel lens   A lens with a surface composed of a series of concentric ribs of stepped cross-sections that make it thinner, lighter, and more efficient than a solid lens.

fuse   Protective device for an electrical circuit to prevent overloading.

gaffer tape   A wide, plasticized cloth tape with many uses in concert production.

gain   The increase in signal power from one point to another.

gel   Color filter. Originally made of gelatin, color filters are now made of plastic.

gobo   A metal stencil placed in the gate of a profile spot to shape the beam of light.

graphic equalizer   An equalizer that has slider-level controls; once set, the sliders represent the response curve.

grid   The framework of trusses from which the lamps are hung.

ground row   Series of lamps in the form of troughs laid on the ground to illuminate a cyclorama or other background.

harmonic distortion   A form of distortion in which unwanted harmonics are added to the original signal.

harmonics   Overtones that are multiples of the fundamental tone that shape the waveform and make it possible to differentiate instruments even when they are playing the same note.

headroom   The space, usually expressed in decibels (dB), between the operating level and the maximum available level. Inadequate headroom distorts transient peaks.

hertz   Hz; the unit of frequency. One hertz equals one cycle per second.

hiss   Noise that sounds like prolonged sibilant sounds.

houselights   Auditorium lighting.

hue   The predominant sensation of color.

hum   Electrical interference caused at mains frequency, 50/60 Hz.

impedance   The degree to which a circuit impedes the flow of an alternating current. Measured in ohms.

induction   Production of current across a space due to electrical or magnetic fields.

infinite bame   Speaker mounting that allows no air paths between front and rear of speaker.

instrument   The general name for lighting fixtures.

intensity of light   The power of a light source, its brightness.

intensity of sound   The objective strength of sound, loudness.

inverse square law   An equation that relates the intensity of light to the distance from the object.

iris   An adjustable circular shutter used in a profile spot to vary the size of the beam.

jack   Terminating point of a circuit. A common term for a phone plug connector.

lamp   A general term for an incandescent light source (bulb, bubble). Also used as a general term for any lighting instrument.

LED   Abbreviation for *light-emitting diode*.

leg   A narrow strip of drape used to mask the sides of the stage.

Leko   A brand of ellipsoidal profile spot.

lighting plot   A scale plan diagram used to indicate the positions and types of lamps used. Details of color, cabling, accessories, patching, and trim height may be included.

limiter   A type of compressor that fixes a ceiling of maximum level without changing the dynamic range below the threshold.

line level   Preamplified signal, in contrast to microphone level. The actual signal levels vary, with nominal microphone level being –50 dBM and nominal line level being +4 dBM.

loudness   The subjective impression of the strength of sound.

luminaire   A complete lighting unit that consists of a lamp with parts designed to distribute the light, position and protect the lamp, and connect the lamp to the power supply.

luminary   A light source.

mask   To conceal the equipment from the audience.

matrix   Electronics for accepting several signals and giving one output.

microphone   A transducer for converting acoustic energy to electrical energy.

MIDI   Acronym for *musical instrument digital interface*.

mirror ball   A spherical ball with a surface covered in small plane mirrors. Multiple moving spots of light shine from the ball when it is lit and rotated.

mixer   The electronics that allow the combination of several signals in desired proportions.

modulation   The control of one waveform by another.

monitor   A speaker cabinet fed with signal to provide the information a performer requires.

multiplexor   Unit for encoding and decoding multiplex signals.

noise   Any unwanted sound.

noise gate   An amplifier that has a zero output until the input level exceeds a chosen threshold level.

nook light   Small, open-fronted trough fitting with a short strip light and curved reflector.

notch filter   An equalizer with a very narrow bandwidth.

octave   The interval between a given tone and its repetition eight tones above or below on the musical scale. A note that is an octave higher than another note is twice the frequency of the first note.

offstage   A position outside the performing area.

omnidirectional microphone   A microphone that is equally sensitive in all directions.

onstage   In the performing area.

open circuit   A circuit that is not continuous and cannot pass any current.

oscillator   A device for producing continuous oscillation or a pure tone at any desired frequency.

oscilloscope   A device for visual display of electronic waveforms.

PA   Abbreviation for *public address system*; an alternative term for *sound system*.

pad   A series of resistors to introduce a fixed amount of gain reduction for impedance-matching purposes.

pan   In lighting: to move the beam of a lamp from side to side of the stage. In sound: to alter the position of a signal laterally.

parametric equalizer   An equalizer that can vary frequency, level, and bandwidth.

par light   A tungsten-halogen (quartz) lamp in which a parabolic aluminized reflector forms part of the bulb. An internally silvered reflector and a molded lens front glass provide a fixed beam. Par bulbs are available in various beam sizes.

patching   Connecting cables in the correct circuits.

phantom power   Method of sending DC supply to a condenser microphone or direct box by connecting the positive side to both signal wires of a balanced line and the negative to the screen.

phase   The position of a waveform at any given instant in the cycle. Waves are in phase when their cycle positions coincide.

pink noise   Pink noise is white noise that has passed through a filter to bring the response to an equal energy level (per octave) as heard by the human ear.

pitch   Subjective effect of sound related mainly to frequency but also affected by intensity and harmonic structure.

potentiometer   A variable resistor used for volume and tone controls. Commonly called a *pot*.

prefade listen   Facility available on mixing consoles for listening to a signal before it is fed to the main program outputs.

presence   Quality of immediacy. Boosting the upper middle frequencies achieves presence.

profile spot   A lamp with a beam that can be either soft or hard.

proscenium   The wall that divides the stage from the auditorium. The opening through which the audience views the stage is called the *proscenium opening*.

pyrotechnics   Any bangs, flashes, or explosions.

RAM   Acronym for *random access memory*. Information that can be memory written in or read out in any order.

recovery time   The time taken for a compressor/limiter to restore the gain to normal when the signal is reduced.

resonance   The tendency of any physical body to vibrate most freely at a particular frequency because of excitation by a sound with that particular frequency.

reverberation   The sustaining effect of multiple sound reflections in an enclosed area.

ribbon microphone   Microphone that uses a thin metal ribbon suspended in a magnetic field.

rig   To install and set up equipment in the required position. The finished assembly of lamps positioned, patched, and focused for a performance.

rostrum   A scenic platform, a riser.

rumble   Low-frequency vibration.

scrim   Thin netting (gauze) used to provide translucent eyes or create scenic diffusion.

set   A group of risers arranged to give a decorative effect.

sightlines   Theoretical lines indicating what the audience can see.

signal to noise   The ratio of the desired signal to residual system noise.

silhouette   A pictorial style that concentrates on subject outline for its effect. Surface detail, tone, texture, and color are suppressed.

silicon chip   A method of fabricating resistors and transistors into miniaturized circuits on a wafer of silicon, which is cased in a plastic or ceramic body with leads bonded onto the silicon.

spanset   An endless loop of nylon strands used for rigging purposes. Because it is a soft sling, the spanset can be used for a variety of rigging applications. Spansets are color coded for weight loading.

special   A light performing a particular function.

spiking   Marking a position on the stage.

strike   To remove a piece of set or equipment from the performing area.

tab   Any curtain.

talkback   Headphone intercom system.

teaser   A border used to mask trusses or fly bars.

threshold   The point above which level changes take place.

throw   The distance from a light to the object being lit.

tilt   The vertical movement of a light.

transformer   Component that has two coils of wire, the primary and secondary, the lengths of which are in a fixed ratio to allow voltages to be stepped up or down and circuit impedances to be matched for maximum power transfer.

translucent   Allowing light to pass through without being transparent.

tree   A high stand or tower with horizontal arms for mounting lamps.

trim   The grid: to level a grid or truss. The dimmers: to adjust dimmer response to control voltage. Dimmers out of trim do not give the subtle control required for stage lighting.

unidirectional microphone   A microphone that is sensitive to sound from one direction only.

upstage   The stage area toward the back, away from the audience.

VCA   Abbreviation for *voltage-controlled amplifier*, used instead of faders to control channel gain in a sound control console.

volt   The unit of electrical force.

VU meter   A meter for indicating program volume that gives signal power, in decibels, on a steady tone and volume units (percentage utilization of the channel) on program.

wavelength   The distance between corresponding parts of a waveform.

white noise   A full audio spectrum signal with the same energy level at all frequencies.

windshield   A foam sock placed over a microphone to reduce the amount of wind amplified. Also called *popshield*.

wings   The areas on either side of the stage.

zero level   The level used for lining up audio equipment. Zero decibels equals 1 milliwatt (mW). This corresponds to 0.775 V runs across a resistance of 600 ohms.

zoom lens   A variable-focus lens.

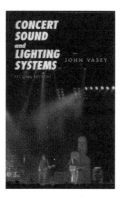

Focal Press

Related Audio Title

Modern Recording Techniques
Fourth Edition
David Miles Huber and
Robert E. Runstein

As the most complete, up-to-date, accurate and authoritative recording guide, this book reflects the latest developments in digital audio and hard-disk recording techniques. It provides in-depth insights into hands-on operation of studio recording equipment, such as project studio, and explores the latest in digital technology, multitrack systems, MIDI, and the electronic musical instrument industry. It is the perfect book for anyone wanting to learn professional recording – producers, musicians, multimedia developers, audio for video professionals, universities, schools, and audio enthusiasts.

David Miles Huber is widely acclaimed in the recording industry as an author, musician, digital audio consultant, engineer, and guest lecturer.

Robert E. Runstein has been associated with all aspects of the recording industry, working as a performer, sound mixer, electronics technician, A & R specialist, and record producer.

Copyright 1997 • 496pp • Paperback • 0-240-80308-6

Visit the Focal Press Web Site at: http://www.bh.com/focalpress

Available from all better book stores or in case of difficulty call:
1-800-366-2665 in the U.S. or +44 1865 310366 in Europe.

Focal Press

Music Technology Series

Sound and Recording: An Introduction
Third Edition
Francis Rumsey and Tim McCormick
April 1997 • 384pp • Paperback • 0-240-51487-4

MIDI Systems and Control
Second Edition
Francis Rumsey
1994 • 256pp • Paperback • 0-240-51370-3

The Audio Workstation Handbook
Francis Rumsey
1996 • 286pp • Paperback • 0-240-51450-5

Digital Audio CD-ROM Tutor Resource
Markus Erne
May 1997 • Compact Disk • 0-240-51502-1

Digital Audio CD-ROM Students Edition
Markus Erne
May 1997 • Compact Disk • 0-240-51501-3

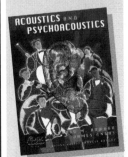

Acoustics and Psychoacoustics
Edited by Francis Rumsey
David Howard and James Angus
1996 • 224pp • Paperback • 0-240-51428-9